Head of the Class

Stories From America's Classrooms

Compiled and edited by Dr. Jim Uhlenkott

Original illustrations by Christa Prentiss

Preface

Teachers in America's public schools are under more scrutiny than at any time in our history. There is a cry for greater accountability, more research-based instruction and more stringent course work. America's schools used to be rated number one in the world. The United States currently ranks 26th in math, 21st in science and 17th in reading. U.S. Education Secretary Arne Duncan says these flat scores are a "…picture of educational stagnation".[1]

Are our classrooms stagnant? What are our teachers doing? Are they not working hard enough? Are they not trained well enough? Are they failing our students?

It is possible that some of these statements, perhaps all of them, are true to some degree somewhere in our schools. They are not the norm, however.

Written by real teachers and students, the stories presented in this book are a testament to the amazing work being done by teachers in our schools. Some of the stories are funny, some are sad. Some tell of incredible challenges being overcome. Others speak to amazing success stories, and some of disappointment. Some are written by teachers about students, and some are written by students about their teachers. All of them, however, highlight the amazing work being done in America's classrooms every day.

These stories are a mere microcosm of reality. They should not be read as a small number of isolated incidents, but rather as a representative of thousands of interactions taking place in schools every day.

---

[1] NBC News, Dec. 3, 2013

I was a public school teacher for 18 years, and have been teaching at the university level for the last 12. My courses in teacher education are filled with young, talented adults, all wanting to enter this challenging, rewarding and ever-evolving profession. They want to make a difference, they want to affect lives, and they want to help others to be successful. They also have questions. Can I do this job? Will I be able to connect with my students? How can I instill a motivation to learn in these young people?

It takes more than knowing the material to be an effective teacher. It takes more than passing teacher education courses and state-mandated exams and evaluations. All of us have had teachers that were experts in their field but were not effective in the classroom. The stories in this book all highlight the true skill needed to make a difference in our schools. Effective teaching begins with caring relationships. Effective teachers touch the hearts of their students. They not only care if you pass their tests, they care about your life.

The purposes of this book are to highlight some of the great things that happen in America's classrooms every day and to bring inspiration and hope to future educators. Our students are in good hands. Their teachers are indeed at the head of the class.

Table of Contents

1. Welcome to Education

By Carol Rasor

Carol Rasor taught resource room, 2nd, 4th and 6th grade, most recently at Farwell Elementary School in Mead, Washington.

> **⚠ WARNING**
>
> It has been determined that teaching may cause anxiety, stress and depression.
> Stop! Declare a different major! If you proceed, remember from this point forward why you are choosing this profession.

This warning label should be on every application for admission into a teacher education program. If you are going into the field of teaching you know you will not receive monetary compensation equal to a highly paid CEO, nor will you receive a bronze plaque in the concrete of a walkway or an award in the Hall of Fame. You are never going to walk the red carpet in front of the news media or stand at a podium to receive an "Oscar" and the accolades of your peers. No, you're more apt to hear nothing more than what seems to be whispered "kudos". Despite what I just said what I really want to say is: **Don't sell yourself short,** if you in fact choose to become a teacher.

Perhaps you, like I, will at some point in your career receive a few acknowledgements from parents or former students and when you do, they will be memorable.

Through the years, I encountered parents of former students who thanked me for having had an impact on their child, but I am here to tell you of three times in particular that I received thanks from students. These three came from students who were the most unlikely to succeed. The first one I remember came from a former 5th grade student. He was a 10 year old boy, who had entered my classroom having been enrolled in the public school system for the first time ever. Up until that year, he had been home schooled. Home schooling was a relatively new endeavor at that time and homeschooled students were typically behind academically. This boy was even more so. Shocked as I was to discover he didn't even know enough to write on a sheet of notebook paper horizontally rather than between the spaces with the lines running vertically, I was pleased to discover, shy as he was, he was also very eager to learn.

Two years later, he must have come over from the middle school and left a note on my desk. It was scrawled on a scrap piece of notebook paper; "Thank you for being such a nice teacher". It was signed and I had to smile.

KK was a student in my class twice, once when I was teaching a first and second grade combination and again the one year I taught 6th grade. KK was struggling in the primary grades and by the time she was in 6th grade I was concerned that she would become a drop-out statistic before the end of junior high.

She came from a dysfunctional family and was running with the wrong crowd. I conducted an experiment in my classroom that year which is too lengthy to explain at this time, but what I do want to share is that the end result proved to be more valuable than I could have anticipated.

I did not learn of the result until twenty some years later, when I received a long letter from KK relating all that had taken place in her life following her 6th grade year in my class. She told of how she had gained the courage to emancipate herself from her family, seeking shelter with her pastor's family, in order to graduate from high school. She went on to college and became a teacher in a school district with a high number of disadvantaged teens. She attributed her success to my teaching and reaching out to her during her last year in the elementary program. I, of course, did not accept credit but told her it was due to her courage and perseverance.

Not until this final encounter did I allow myself to think that we teachers may in fact play an important role in the lives of young people. My husband and I were hosting a Christmas party in our home for the 12 employees of his business. By this time I had been out of teaching for 2 years and was now working as the office manager and secretary for my husband. All who had gathered were enjoying the evening when a young employee in his late twenties said he had something he wanted to share. In fact, he said he had wanted to share this for some time, but was trying to find the "right" place and time. He proceeded to announce that I had been the reason he had learned to read. He had been placed in my resource room when he was in second grade. He went on to say that he had hated school and had lacked any confidence until that year. He caught me by surprise as he had changed greatly from age 8 to age 28. His last name had also changed when his mother remarried when he was younger, perhaps explaining why I had not realized who he was, not to mention the fact that we were both now living in Washington rather than Idaho. He thanked me and gave me the credit for any success he had experienced over the years.

It was after this that I began to evaluate my 20 years of teaching differently. I then realized that while we as teachers never equate ourselves or our profession with scientists, doctors, engineers or lawyers, we need to keep in mind we influence the young minds that go on to become scientists, doctors, engineers, lawyers and teachers. We need to appreciate the fact that we help to influence the young minds that become well-adjusted, contributing citizens. More importantly we are more closely related to doctors than we think, for we too save lives. We may be the reason an individual does not end up in prison, homeless and on the street or in abject poverty. What better legacy can we leave the upcoming generations? So, I will say it again: Do not sell yourself short. The field of education may be underappreciated, underfunded and undervalued, but I'm here to say welcome to a worthwhile profession. Good luck!

2. The Real Lesson

By Dr. Jim Uhlenkott

Jim Uhlenkott taught in the Mead School District for 18 years.

    A new school year is an exciting time.   The month of August, still in the heart of summer and all the activities that go with that, always brought me an anticipation of the new school year.   It was exciting to see my new class list, go to my room, begin preparations, and think of all the wonderful adventures the new school year would bring. Perhaps I was more excited than my students.

Fourth grade was my teaching assignment that year. It was my second time teaching this grade level so I looked forward to the challenge, having one year under my belt already. Fourth grade is a dramatic change from third grade, my previous teaching assignment. The students in fourth grade are more mature and ready for stronger challenges academically. My lessons would have to reflect this.

I was still a relatively young teacher, this being my sixth year, but I was much more confident in both my teaching skills and in my main area of expertise, literacy. I had worked as a Title 1 reading teacher my first two years out of college, had obtained my Master's degree in literacy and felt good about my work at the elementary level so far. My comfort level was heightened because I was a veteran teacher in this school and knew many of the students and their families now, having had several of their older brothers and sisters in my classes previously.

Adding to all this, I was going to have Cory in my class. Cory's older sister had been in my class the year before, so I had gotten to know the family well. They were a wonderful family and I truly enjoyed working with them. Cory was a child with special needs, especially in any area related to language: reading and writing chief among them. This was perfect as literacy was my area of expertise and I looked forward to helping Cory become a stronger reader and writer. I knew I could help him.

The school year began well. It was a good group of students; they were well-behaved, worked hard, and a lot of fun. This was going to be a good year.

My work with Cory began as I anticipated. I diagnosed his reading abilities, formulated a plan of remediation and we embarked down the road to improvement. It was slow going, as I predicted. Reading skills are not changed overnight, especially when there are special needs to consider. No one in my class worked harder than Cory. No one was more well-liked, either.

Cory had an amazing capacity to care for others. His concern for his classmates was genuine and tangible. He was not necessarily on their level socially, but it didn't matter. Everyone loved him.

The year marched onward and Cory's improvement in literacy was not what I was hoping it would be, and I found myself becoming frustrated. This frustration was not at Cory; he was doing everything right. He worked hard, had an amazing attitude and did everything that was asked of him. My frustration was with myself. I thought I would be able to bring him further along and do it more quickly. It bothered me that it wasn't happening the way I was hoping.

I began to research more, going through my materials and textbooks from college, looking for things that I had possibly missed or that I could do differently. I even contacted my literacy professors from college, asking them for advice and direction. These efforts brought me more areas to try, more techniques to employ, but Cory still did not progress. What was I doing wrong?

Sometime in the late winter, perhaps February, it began to get to me. I was failing Cory. He was still an amazing boy, a hard worker with a great attitude, loved by his classmates, but I was not helping him become a better reader. This "failure" was even harder because this was in my area of strength. It was starting to get to me and it all came to a head one night as I arrived home after school.

I pulled in the driveway, got out of the car and headed into the house. I felt like the worst teacher in the world and evidently it showed. I closed the door behind me, walked into the kitchen and sort of stood there, not able to find any motivation to even take my coat off or say hello. My wife looked at me and immediately said, "Jim, what's wrong?"

Standing there in our kitchen, my coat still on, my shoulders sagging, I could not find the words to answer her. Tears formed in my eyes and all I could say was, "Cory's not getting it!" Tears flowed down my face and I leaned my head against one of the kitchen cupboards and cried. Eventually I pulled myself together and attempted to "leave school at school". The evening went on as I tried to be a good dad and husband, but probably not succeeding very well at either one. Mercifully, the day came to an end and I went to bed and tried to sleep.

The alarm clock rang as it always did, having no understanding or mercy for my frayed emotions. The snooze button bore the brunt of my still-fragile state and I lay there, thinking...

I don't want to do this.
I don't have to do this.

I did not go into this profession to fail; I became a teacher to make a difference, to help people, and I'm not. I'm failing Cory.

I'll call in sick. It won't matter. Let some substitute teacher be there today. It won't matter anyway. They will probably do a better job than I am.

What was my real motivation for becoming a teacher? I ask my current teacher-education students this same question at the beginning of every semester. Their answers are almost always the same...

"I want to make a difference."
"I just really like children."
"I want to help others be successful."

There is nothing wrong with these answers. There is something wrong if you are going into education and you don't feel these things. These are just the beginning, however. This is the starting point. The motivation for teaching must go beyond these answers. There must be something deeper that will drive us to continue forward though the difficulties and obstacles that are part of every classroom. A deep motivation for our students and for teaching must be found in the midst of the problems and chaos. Without it, we may hear the alarm go off, hit the snooze button, and say to ourselves the things I was saying that morning...

I'll call in sick.
It won't matter.

It often, perhaps usually, takes time and experience to find this place. I hadn't found it yet.

As I continued to lie in my bed, it dawned on me that Cory was teaching me a lesson. He was teaching me that my motivation was all wrong. I wasn't motivated to help others, to guide them and help them grow, mature and learn. I was motivated by my success, and I defined that success by how well my students did.

Cory's motivation, on the other hand, was much more pure. He was motivated to do his best, to work hard every day and to care for others. He was motivated to always be there, every day, no matter how he felt, and to bring joy into the room with him. His worth as a person wasn't based on someone else's success. He knew he was valued and he tried to make others feel valued as well.

So I got up, got dressed, and went to work.

Nothing amazing happened that day. Nothing amazing happened the rest of the year. It was work as usual. The students were still fun to be around, they still worked hard, we had some fun class times and some challenging ones. I tried to be creative and engaging, and Cory still didn't improve. He never really improved in any area of literacy.

Cory was, however, a great success.

He was a success because he made the very best of his abilities.

He was a success because he impacted those around him, and he did this for the rest of his life.

He was a success because he loved people, and they felt this love from him.

He was a success because he never quit. Not once.

Cory taught me my greatest lesson about being a teacher. Here was a young boy with some serious learning issues, yet he never had a bad attitude, he never quit, he never even looked frustrated. All he did was work hard, treat people well and enjoy life. I want to be like him. I want to work hard, do my job to the best of my abilities and continue to improve as a teacher. I want to treat people well and make them feel like the special human beings they are. Like Cory, I want to enjoy life. All of it. The successes and the difficulties are all worth savoring. It is in these moments that real lessons are learned and real life is lived. The joy of teaching is not just found in good grades, high test scores or even fun activities. The real joy of teaching is found in the struggles.

I have several college degrees and received great training in my educational career, but the greatest lesson I learned was from a young boy in the fourth grade.

Thank you Cory.

3. Getting "Fired"

By Don Kardong

Don Kardong is a former Olympic runner and the founder of the Spokane Lilac Bloomsday Run, one of the largest timed road races in the United States.

I was a sixth grade classroom teacher for three years, from 1974 through 1977, long enough to get a good taste of the frustration all teachers feel when they can't seem to get through to certain students, maybe most students, but in retrospect I also remember the success stories, the kind of thing that just might override some of that ongoing frustration.

One of these resulted when three of the students, let's call them Fred, Bill and Dave to protect the innocent, asked me if they could start a class newspaper. Actually, as I found out later, it was Fred's idea. He shared his idea with Bill and Dave, and it was those two who came to me asking if they could spearhead the effort. Both were great students, so I told them if they kept up with the rest of their classwork, which I knew they would, it would be fine.

In no time Bill and Dave had christened themselves co-editors and set up their "offices" in one corner of the room, and had hired some of the other students, including Fred, to write articles. I was curious to see how this would play out, because Fred was a student who almost never got his work done. Cajoling, enticing, threatening, and any and all other attempts to get him to produce work went unfulfilled. I found this especially frustrating because he was clearly a clever kid, someone who should have had no trouble keeping up with the curriculum. I suggested to his mother that she have Fred tested for attention deficit disorder, but was told later that the results were negative, so bottom line, I had a smart kid who, for whatever reason, couldn't complete class assignments. So it was with some real interest that I watched to see how Fred would do as a reporter for the class newspaper.

About a week into the project, Editor Bill approached me during a break. He was clearly dejected. "We've got a problem," he said.

"What's the problem?" I countered, half expecting the answer.

"Well," he said, "We're almost ready to print our first paper, but we can't do it until we get Fred's article, and we've asked a bunch of times but he still hasn't turned it in."

"That's an interesting problem," I responded.

"So what are we supposed to do? We can't print the paper until we get his article."

"Well, if you were the editor of a real paper and your reporter didn't get his assignment done, what would you do?"

Bill's answer was exactly what I was hoping for. "I'd fire him."

"OK then," I said. "Go fire him."

A minute later Fred approached my desk. The look on his face was priceless. He was incredulous.

"What's the matter, Fred?" I said, feigning ignorance.

"Mr. Kardong," he whined, "Bill fired me."

"Really," I replied, "Why'd he do that?"

"He said I didn't turn in my article."

"Did you?"

"No, but the newspaper was my idea."

"Fred, you're a reporter for a newspaper and you didn't do your assignment. That will get a reporter fired."

"But I still want to be on the newspaper."

"Well, if I were you'd I'd go finish my assignment, take it to your editor, and beg to get your job back."

Fred mulled that over for a second, and then headed back to his desk. I learned later that he completed the article and managed to get his job back. It may very well have been the only assignment he completed all year.

I have been asked if this lesson sank in, and if I know how Fred has fared as an adult. Unfortunately, I don't know. What I do know is that he was bright, and with the right motivation he could definitely get his work done. I hope that getting "fired" in sixth grade was a lesson good enough to last a lifetime.

4. The Notorious Seven

By Jerad Farley

Jarad Farley is a fifth grade teacher at Wahitis Elementary School in Othello, Washington

I love the first day of school. Through my formative years, I never lost the incredible feeling you get when you walk in on the first day of school with a backpack full of new supplies to see friends and faces that have curiously not existed in your world during the summer months. Sometimes, I wonder if that may be a large part of my decision to become a teacher. Maybe, in my inner psyche, I just couldn't give up that wonderful feeling that only a fresh start each September can provide. I mean, what other career affords you that kind of opportunity. This new-year zeal has always triggered a desire on my part to get back in the building as soon as possible to set up my classroom. As soon as I received my keys I'd begin spending hours setting things in my room just right.

One day, in my third year of teaching, I was busily putting my room together when a colleague happened to stop in as I was writing out student nametags and placing them on desks. My colleague walked around the room and began to notice and recognize the names of the students that would be walking through my door in just a few short weeks, making comments like, "Oh, you have her. She's such a nice girl", and "You're lucky to have him, he's very bright". These remarks floated by and seemed the stuff of small talk until her tone changed (cue the dun, dun, dunnn). I began to hear, "oh no, he is always in trouble", "look out for this boy, he has no respect for teachers", "this kid doesn't have any parental support, good luck getting him to do his work". By the time she was done, I counted seven boys that, according to her, needed to be sent to boarding school or some other institution that could appropriately address their behavioral needs. She wished me good luck and advised me to get with the counselor and previous teachers right away to determine appropriate discipline plans for these boys. All this and I hadn't even met the students yet.

I felt overwhelmed and that night I went home utterly deflated. I talked with my wife and wondered what I was getting myself into. I had done fairly well the previous two years in my teaching but now I was worried. Was I adequately equipped to handle this group of students, these "notorious seven" boys this year? This colleague had me legitimately questioning whether or not I was going to make it through the first week of school, let alone a whole year. I didn't sleep well that night or any other night for the next couple of weeks.

The first day of school arrived, ready or not, and I stood by the door, as I always did, ready to shake the hand of each fresh new face that walked in my room. This is one of my favorite moments of the whole year, getting to see the excited faces of the kids that will become part of my school family. However, I wasn't enjoying this moment as much as I normally do. The preconceived notions that I had developed about these seven boys colored my outlook in that otherwise happiest of times. Each boy that held out his hand to me left me wondering: is this one of the seven? Is this one of the boys that was going to make my life miserable? I was constantly bracing myself for something to happen, some telltale sign that this was indeed a child to approach with caution, but they didn't seem all that terrifying. In fact, shaking their hands and looking into their faces they looked just like regular, happy kids. I took a deep breath and began instructing the students in the procedures and expectations for our class. By the end of the day, I had no major disruptions and as I set out for my car to head home I had put the whole notion of the class from hades out of my mind. The honeymoon period, however, was about to end.

The days progressed and I found myself dealing with behavior after behavior: shouting in class, fighting on the playground, not turning in homework, not following class procedures, talking in class, just to name a few. I began to notice that these seven boys were creating the culture of my classroom and it was a culture that, if left unchecked, would soon turn toxic and they were bringing the other students down with them. So, I did what any good teacher would do, I enforced my rules and expectations even stronger. These boys began spending time with me at recess, getting phone calls home, losing privileges in class, etc… Now, the days began to turn into weeks and much to my surprise, things were still the same. These boys stayed in for recesses, got phone calls home, lost privileges and nothing changed. I didn't know what to do. I remember telling my wife on one particularly difficult day that I didn't know if I could see myself getting through the year.

It was during this time of despair on a Saturday morning in early October that I happened to glance at my bookshelf and noticed a book that I had purchased for one of my courses during college. Like many college students I had never really read the book beyond completing a few assignments, but now it seemed to be staring at me begging to be read. The book was Harry Wong's "The First Days of School". I read the book cover to cover that very same day. It spoke to me much like it has countless other educators since its publication. There are many great lessons and sound advice for teachers in this book, but I pulled out one big idea that seemed like a possible solution to my classroom troubles. Like many great ideas it is simple really, but also quite profound. What if I just told students what I expected of them and then expected it? Such a straightforward concept but one that would take more thinking and work to implement than any other idea I have ever practiced in the classroom. I wasn't sure it would work, but I was willing to try anything.

That Monday, I had a talk with the entire class. I started by saying that there would be no more punishment in the classroom. No more having to stay in at recess, no more calls home for disruptive classroom behavior, no more heads down on desks. The students were in disbelief and immediately several hands shot up (mostly from the notorious seven). I told them that I would communicate what I expected for every activity or procedure in class and that I would expect them to perform it. I then met individually with each of the seven boys to restate my earlier points and ask if there was any further clarification needed. I made each of them aware that I cared too much about them to allow them to continue on their present course of action in the classroom. I wanted to see each one of them succeed.

I would like to say that change happened overnight. It didn't. There was much the students had to learn to live in this new system and much I had to learn from them to make it work. It wasn't until January of that year that we had made our way completely out of the messiness of that year's rocky start. Ultimately, discipline and classroom management came down to a few simple ideas administered in a consistent and equitable manner. If a student didn't do their homework, I would have a private chat with them about it. I'd remind them of the expectation and let them know that I expected to see their assignment the next day. If a student shouted out in class, I would discreetly whisper in their ear and remind them of the expectation. Any behavior contrary to the accepted classroom expectations was addressed privately with a simple reminder of what I expected of them. Slowly but surely behaviors declined. Homework turn-in rates went up, and classroom disruptions were at a minimum.

The important point here is that discipline was handled privately, to honor the student's dignity, and it was handled consistently. I could never let one thing slip. Any misbehavior that I let slide would cause a chink in the armor of our classroom structure. Trust me, students were always watching. If I was aware of the behavior, I had to address it. By the end of the year our rate of return for homework was 100%. There was not one single missing assignment in the grade book for any student (that encompassed the entire third trimester grading period). Additionally, not one member of the seven was suspended that year: remarkable considering every one of them had served some form of suspension in each of their previous grades. This was also the last school year that I ever wrote a disciplinary referral. I never needed to again. What started out as one of the worst years of my professional life ended up being one of the best. The relationships I built with these students were so rich and so much deeper because of the fundamental shift I made in the way I viewed kids.

Looking back and reflecting on that year and those seven boys, I realize that quite possibly they never expected much of themselves. I believe the majority of their behaviors stemmed from this inner belief. They needed someone to believe in them and for them. Having high expectations and then holding each student accountable to those expectations showed a deep level of commitment on my behalf that no amount of indoor recess could ever accomplish. It is easier, in my opinion, to tell a misbehaving student to stay in for recess than to individually address their behavioral needs. Personally engaging the student around the cause of disruption opens a dialogue between the teacher and the student and sends a message of caring to that child. Once the students learned that they could do the right things and exhibit the characteristics appropriate for success, internalization of the new behaviors began to take place. They began to believe in themselves.

It has been several years since the "notorious seven" was in my room. I have followed the educational paths of most of my students and certainly of those seven. Each one is doing well in school and I'd like to believe that what we learned that year has something to do with it. In fact, I recently received a letter from one of the particularly infamous members of the seven. He thanked me for believing in him and teaching him that he was an intelligent, capable student who could succeed. This student, as well as the rest of the class from that year, taught me to fundamentally believe in high expectations for all kids no matter their poor reputation.

I was influenced by the well-meaning comments of my colleagues, and allowed them to taint how I viewed and treated these seven boys. It wasn't the students who needed to change, it was my own beliefs and the way I viewed discipline that had to profoundly change before I could help those kids work towards their full potential. The "notorious seven" weren't so notorious after all.

5. That's a Teacher!

By Dr. Jim Uhlenkott

Jim Uhlenkott taught in the Mead School District for 18 years.

Hillyard is a poor section of my home town of Spokane, Washington, but it was not always that way. From the 1930s to the early 1960s, Hillyard was a booming hub of commerce and activity fueled by the Great Northern Railroad and all the jobs that came with it. The Great Northern was centered in Hillyard and not only did all the passenger and freight trains pass through this small community but this is where they were fueled and maintained. Thousands of men and women worked for the railroad, including my dad.

Slowly, travel by air and car became more convenient, goods were shipped more by truck than by rail, and the railroad industry began to dwindle. I went to elementary school at St. Patrick's Catholic school in Hillyard when the railroad decline was just beginning. Hillyard was still vibrant, but it was losing steam quickly, along with railroad industry. Poverty had begun to set in and some 30 years later this would the poorest zip code in our state.

Hillyard, being a blue-collar area, produced blue-collar families: hard-working, no-frills, families that loved their kids and worked hard to provide for them. The students at St. Pats were good kids for the most part, but we were definitely on the lower end of the socio-economic scale even then, and it showed. We didn't think about going to college to become a doctor, lawyer or CPA; we thought about maybe graduating from high school. Many of my classmates were in trouble with the police or juvenile authorities at one point or another. Fights on the playground were common place. St. Pat's was run by the Sisters of the Holy Names and almost every class was taught by one of these nuns. Class sizes were large and so were the problems. My class, from first grade to eighth, usually had over thirty kids in it, with my seventh grade class having 36. Into this setting walked a new teacher; a young woman, having only recently taken her vows to be a member of the Sisters of the Holy Names, Sister Lois Marie.

Sister Lois Marie was a tall woman, easily five feet, eleven inches tall, and towered over us seventh graders. She was an imposing figure in her dark, flowing habit, and we were a little intimidated as she walked in the room that first morning. It was clear that she was in charge of this class, not us, and we were not sure if we wanted to challenge this commanding educator.

The morning of that first day went without incident; we were all on our best behavior as we tried to get a read on our new teacher. St. Pat's was set up with self-contained classrooms from first grade all the way through eighth, and as such we still had recesses. Morning recess time arrived that first day and we all headed out to the playground and into the warm September weather. Our class was on the second floor of the building but instead of walking out to the hallway, then down the steps and out the doors of the building, we always went out the fire escape. It was faster, made for less people clogging up the hallways, and, more importantly, it looked cooler. I carried the football out to recess that morning as that was our favorite game. Like most seventh grade boys, our evaluation of our athletic prowess was slightly exaggerated.

Walking down the fire escape we couldn't help but notice that "Sister" was walking out with us, right down the fire escape. This made no sense! Why was she coming? The nuns didn't do recess duty; we had parent volunteers for that, so why was she following us? We got to the bottom of the stairs and as I turned to go with my buddies I heard Sister's voice behind me.

"Hey Jim, throw me the ball."

What? Why would she want me to throw her the ball? This was a huge waste of our time. Recess was only 15 minutes long and we didn't have time for some woman to want to look at our football. We were serious, fledgling athletes! We needed to get going here! I complied, however, tossing her the ball and just hoping she would hurry up and throw it back.

"Go out," she said.

Go out? Now she's really wasting our time! I took a few token steps and turned around with a look on my face that said, come on lady, just throw me the ball.

"No," she said, "go out!"

Fine! You want me to go out, I'll go out, and I turned and took off running. This will be a waste of time but I was going to show her that she was in way over her head here! I sprinted down the black top, looked over my shoulder, and couldn't believe what I saw. Sister Lois Marie, in her long, flowing robes, dropped back, planted her back foot, brought the football right up next to her ear, transferred all of her weight to her front foot and threw a bullet! This ball was on a rope! It sailed, no rocketed, to me and I caught it, and it almost took the wind out of me. As I stood there, this football still impaled in my midsection, I looked up at her and had one thought: That's a Teacher!

She came out to play football with us and we immediately named her all-time QB. She was the quarterback for both teams, as none of us could throw like she could. It was a badge of honor to catch one of her laser throws and not drop it. She came out to recess a lot that year. She didn't always of course, but a lot, and as she became our favorite quarterback, she also became our favorite teacher.

It takes more than being able to throw a football to be a good teacher. Sister cared for us, and we knew it. She took no guff from any of us, but always treated us with respect, like we mattered. She refused to settle for anything less than our best and wasn't afraid to get right in our faces when we wanted to settle for it. She came to every one of our football games, basketball games and baseball games. She listened to our stories, cared when we were hurting and understood our fragile, hormone-based emotions.

She taught us how to really study and apply ourselves. She made us believe that we were capable and could accomplish good things. She was also a very good teacher. It was watching her teach her lessons in math, history and all the other subjects that I began to think that maybe I could do that. Maybe I could teach. It is because of Sister that I became a teacher.

Years later, working with my own elementary students, I found myself doing things in class that I learned as a student in 7th grade. I emulated many of Sister's classroom management and pedagogical techniques. I also found myself going out to recess a lot.

Sister Lois Marie was our teacher for both our seventh and eighth grade years. She didn't live long enough to see us grow up or even graduate from high school. She died of a brain aneurism when we were in tenth grade. I would like for her to have seen me teach. I would have liked to have her watch me and give me suggestions on how I could improve. Mostly, I would like her to know that she was my inspiration to become a teacher.

Sister Lois Marie: That's a Teacher!

6. Perspective Is In the Eye of the Beholder

By Mark Kondo

Mark Kondo is a retired English teacher, counselor and wrestling coach at Othello High School, Othello, Washington.

We educators realize the importance of higher education. Attending high school, I knew I would attend college and hopefully get a masters' degree or even more. Raising our children there was no question of if they would attend college, but where they would go. Both of our children are educators and have earned master's degrees. Already, when my three and five year old granddaughters are given money for their piggy banks and you ask them what the money is for, they reply, "For college!" I am working on getting them to add, "I am going to the University of Washington," (my alma mater).

I started my education career in Spokane as an English teacher at Ferris High School where many students had parents who were professionals. Later, I worked as a counselor at Shadle Park High School where the students were mainly middle class. Students in both schools were geared toward attending college and pursuing a post high school education.

My wife and I moved to the Columbia Basin 12 years later and worked at a private Christian youth ranch for approximately four years. I then decided to return to education and was able to obtain a job as a counselor at Othello High School. Othello is in the center of Washington State and is primarily a farming and orchard community. The socio-economic makeup of Othello is about 70% Hispanic and poverty is a very real presence in the lives of many students.

My position as a counselor at Othello High School enabled me to enjoy working with the students who had similarities to the students I worked with in Spokane. The students were friendly and enjoyed school activities and just being teenagers. Of course, as an educator and specifically, as a counselor, I encouraged students to understand the value of education and to strive to attend college.

There were two counselors at the high school and each of us worked with specific grade levels. For example, one had the freshmen and juniors and the other had sophomores and seniors. About my second year at Othello High School, I was in charge of the seniors. At the beginning of the year, I issued an "Endangered Species" list. This was a confidential list of seniors who were hovering on the bubble for graduation because of their lack of credits. It was meant to help teachers be aware of students who needed close monitoring to help ensure their graduation.

At the midterm for the first semester, I received a list of those students who had D's and F's. I immediately compared this list with my "Endangered Species" list to see which students I needed to talk to. For one particular student, there was no room for error. She had to pass all her classes in order to graduate.

I sent for the student and offered her a seat in my counseling office. Thinking I could help her to see the logic in making a change to pass all her classes, I proceeded to explain.

"I received a list of students who are not passing classes and you are on the list. You have 2 or 3 Fs. If you don't pass all your classes, you won't graduate. If you don't graduate, you won't be able to go to college. If you don't go to college, you won't be able to get a good job." It seemed very simple, very logical and I expected the student to see the soundness of my argument for making a change in order to successfully pass all her classes.

Waiting for her to respond, I saw tears begin to well up in her eyes. I hoped my argument had been so persuasive that she was moved emotionally and understood the importance of the situation.

Finally, she spoke, "Mr. Kondo, I just want to be the first person in my family to graduate from high school." It was a simple statement that hit me like a ton of bricks. I had just assumed all students wanted to attend college...at least most in the previous high schools where I worked had wanted to.

It made me realize that my perspective and paradigm was not necessarily the same as those of my students. Going to college was a "given" in my world. It was what we did. We went to high school, then on to college to pursue our career of choice. This conversation helped me to see my students in a different light. This young girl in my office had never thought about going to college. Graduating high school would be a great accomplishment in her eyes and in the eyes of her family. I began to realize the importance of truly understanding the shoes my students walk in, and I developed a greater empathy for them and their lives.

This was the first time I had heard a student say they wanted to be the first in their family to graduate from high school. Through the years, I heard it many more times. And then when I truly started to listen, I heard students say "Maybe I could be the first in my family to attend college", or, "I want to be the first in my family to graduate from college."

Later, I had a student who just missed graduating. I encouraged her to finish the one course she needed. She did not get it done the year after she was supposed to graduate, so I kept encouraging her and finally, two years later she made it. When I see her around town, she is always quick to smile and say hello.

The opportunity to help instill dreams in young people or to help them reach for their dreams is what makes working in education a unique and rewarding experience, but to do so we must first listen to them and understand the world in which they live. Their perspective is just that: theirs. They live unique and different lives in unique and different worlds. The real work of teaching is not to get our students to see the world from our perspective. We have to try to see that world through their eyes.

7. A Special Bond

By Kelly Walters

Kelly Walters is a science teacher at North Central High School in Spokane, Washington.

We couldn't have been more different. Brian was a black, 14-year-old, fireplug of muscle layered on top of muscle. I was a white, tall, skinny, bald science teacher.

Brian was from a single-parent home in the east side, in a run-down neighborhood. My parents were both teachers and I grew up on the north side of town, with wide streets, manicured lawns and new homes.

Brian was an extrovert, popping with energy. He liked to tease, often with the phrase "It's because I'm black isn't it?"

Brian struggled in school, especially math. He used to say, "Math and I just don't get along."

I was more of an introvert. I liked to read, write and always loved math and science.

Brian's older brother was in a gang.

My older brother was a dentist.

However, in the fall of 1998, our paths intersected for 55 minutes a day.

Despite all of his academic deficiencies, Brian definitely had personality. This was good and bad. He was funny and likeable. He would also play the part of the class clown, interrupting me with clever comments or absurd questions. Some teachers get frustrated with off-task comments and behavior. I usually like to kind of roll with it. Brian was the kind of kid that made teaching fun for me – or at least interesting. He would often hang around before or after class and talk about sports or just ask if there were going to be any explosions that day (actually a legitimate question in my class). He was one of those kids that you know his name the second day, partially because you keep calling on him to sit down or turn around or stop talking.

Part of the reason that I took a special interest in Brian was because he was an athlete - not the refined "been to all the camps and my dad is my coach" type of athlete, but a raw specimen of power, speed and coordination. This was important to me, in part because I wanted to find a place where Brian could succeed and find an identity, but also because I just so happened to be the boy's track coach. Our team was weak and I was on an all-out assault to try to recruit actual athletes, especially some with power, speed and coordination. Turning out for track would be good for Brian, I reasoned. It would also be good for the track team, which made it even better. So, without much resistance, Brian turned out for our team and suddenly I wasn't limited to a mere 55 minutes a day with him.

One of our first days in practice we did a mini-decathlon, testing kids in different events. Brian was clearly one of our top kids. Brian could develop into a significant scorer for our team, perhaps even a state placer someday. That is, if we could get him academically eligible.

At the end of the first week of practice we took a day off to do a combination of fundraising and community service events. We divided the team into several different crews. Each crew took a different part of the neighborhood and cleaned up garbage on the sidewalks and streets. Each coach supervised a different crew. Brian was assigned to the crew supervised by our pole-vault coach, a 70 year old man who was also my father. The task was not glamorous. Picking up garbage off the street was not every kid's idea of a good time. Some boys grumbled. Some did as little as possible. Brian, on the other hand, jumped into it without hesitation. He was a leader. He took some pride in being a part of the team and cleaning up the neighborhood. Brian thought it was cool to do "good". He worked hard, joked around and acted like it was fun.

Unfortunately, Brian also got in trouble easily. He had a hot temper and a short fuse. One day in my class he got upset about something. As I recall, he got in a conflict with another student and started telling him off very loudly. I asked him to settle down and be quiet, but he just got more agitated. I ended up asking him to go out in the hall and I still remember him telling me and the class to f*** off. I followed him out into the hall where I told him to go to the office. I don't remember exactly what happened after that, but he never returned to my class. As far as I knew, he had dropped out of school entirely.

I didn't hear from him until the next year. My mom and dad had spotted him working at McDonalds. They recognized each other and my parents tried to talk him into going back to school. It took a while, but after attending an alternative school, Brian came back to North Central High School and back onto our track team.

Brian had become bigger, stronger and faster. He made an immediate impact on the team as one of our fastest sprinters and our best jumper. Brian loved being on the team and was funnier than ever. He also drove the coaches crazy. Brian was willing to work hard - to a point. Beyond the point that it made sense to him, however, he would start whining, which turned to arguing, which then resulted in a refusal to finish the workout.

Andre, our sprint coach, was one of the best motivators on the staff. He possessed great charisma and athletes would do anything for him. Andre never got rattled and was always a picture of positive energy, but Brian could get under his skin. One day, after Brian refused to finish the workout that he thought "was stupid," Andre threw up his hands. He came over to me and said, "I give up. You do something with him."

I didn't really know what to do either. I explained to Brian that he put us coaches in a bind. If we just let him out of the workout, then we couldn't expect any one else to finish it either. I told him that if he wanted to compete in the next meet he was somehow going to have to finish the workout. He had several 200 m sprints left to do. By this time everyone had left. I offered to run the 200 m repeats with him and take him home since his ride had already left. Perhaps because I was an "old man," who was going to experience the pain with him, he decided to finish the workout and he competed in the next meet.

Brian ran 2 years for us and ended up graduating on time. On the day of his graduation, he was thrilled to be in his cap and gown. For some kids this is just a right-of-passage and they yawn through both pomp and circumstance. This was truly an accomplishment for Brian. His family was there, a few friends, an older man who had worked with Brian through the Big Brothers program and, of course, my dad and me. Never afraid of emotion, Brian gave everyone hugs and held on long enough to let us know that we were appreciated. This was clearly a day that he thought might never come.

After graduating, Brian jumped around between different low paying jobs, including one stint as a bouncer. Without a question, Brian was not the sort of guy that you wanted to be "bounced" by. He took some community college classes, but he kept tripping up on his old nemesis, "math". One job that he somehow fell into was coaching an "exchange team" that competed in Australia. This was one of those "athletic tours" that was mostly a money-maker for the company that sponsored it, but Brian took it on like he was coaching the Olympic team. He recruited athletes from all over the state and poured his heart and soul into preparing "his team".

The next year, I was looking for someone to help me coach the high jump. We decided to hire Brian, with a small stipend, thinking not only that he could help us, but the responsibility might help him also. He was enthusiastic, faithful, and added some personality to our staff. Sometimes however, he got a little frustrated with the kids. I distinctly remember one time he came to me ready to blow a gasket.

"Coach," he said. "I don't know how you do it." "What do you mean?" I asked. "I told Justin to do 10 run-throughs and he refused," Brian said, "and he told me that his approach was good, so he didn't think he needed to do it 10 times". "Wow," I said. "He actually refused to finish a workout? How dare he?"

Brian was about to ask what sort of punishment I would lay down for the kid, when he saw the smirk on my face.

"I remember an athlete like that a few years ago…" I said. Brian got it. "Yeah, how did you put up with me coach?" he said. We had a good laugh and then walked over to talk to his athlete.

Brian decided to go into the Marines. I had seen him mature over the years, but was a little concerned whether or not he would handle the discipline of the military. If he had trouble doing a set of 200m sprints for Coach Wicks, how was he going to deal with his drill sergeant?

He not only succeeded in boot camp, he excelled. He was selected among 700 new recruits as the top marine in the company. They give a special honor for one standout in the whole camp and they chose Brian Washington.

Brian has continued to grow and thrive. He now has two children and pours out his abundant energy and personality into his wife and kids. You'll never meet a more excited father.

Brian and I were worlds apart when we first met each other in that school classroom. Now we share something that is not often talked about in education journals. We share a bond of love forged over years of shared needs, struggles, and victories. And when my wife gets a call for Mother's Day, it is from a kid that her husband kicked out of class 15 years ago.

8. The Lesson in the Parking Lot

By Anne Wilcox

Anne Wilcox is a Professor of Education at Whitworth University.

He was a gang leader - that is all I knew. On second thought, I knew one more thing. He had been kicked out of three other high schools. So, what would he be like? How would I help other students reach the standards of proficiency in Sophomore English with him in the class? I could tell that I was frightened by the violence in his past. I was also frightened by what others had not been able to do in order to exist with him in the same school. How can we as teachers repair hearts that have known such violence and such rejection?

I was prepared for his huge stature. I was prepared for his defiant look. I was also prepared for the way others stood back from him. But I was not prepared for his poetry.

The English teacher before me had helped this young man find his voice through poetic expression. His style was completely unique. The meter and rhyme were like nothing I had experienced before. It flowed from the language and music of his cultural identity. Faith, family, and music converged to create imagery and theme. The integration of unique cadence and suffering deepened his verse. Though the lines were effective to read, it was when he read his own work that others stopped everything to listen. Maybe that's what transformed him, someone finally listened.

I was told that the year before he had been chosen to read his poetry at the opening of our city's art museum. Apparently, there he stood - the gang leader right beside the mayor. People listened that day in a new way. It was also said that he read in a new way. The tension of a life of violence fell away and the poet emerged. Listeners were spell-bound.

So, now I was his teacher. What would I do on the shoulders of such a discovery? At least he was here - not expelled like so many other times. At least he had discovered through the wisdom and skill of a former English teacher that he had a voice - a unique way to capture our human failings and joys. But what would I do with him?

As the bell rang and students entered the classroom it was easy to spot him. The scars, visible and invisible, were evident by his gate and by the avoidance of others. The class was working long and hard with the novel, "To Kill a Mockingbird." He knew better than the other students about the isolation that comes when one is different mentally, physically, culturally, and linguistically.

After a few class sessions, he cautiously offered me a poem that explored killing the innocent and the killing of innocence. As I thanked him, he turned to go. I stopped him with these words, "I think poetry is a lot like music. Besides reading this to myself, I'd really like to hear you read it out loud the way it is supposed to be read. It would mean even more if I could hear you read what you have created."

I had heard about his poetry; now I was able to hear his poetry. I was so moved by the content and so moved by the sound that emanated from this hard, young man that tears began. I risked letting him see them.

The next day he was at my classroom door at the end of the day. He offered to carry my books and supplies to the car. An act of kindness from a gang leader? For several days he did the same thing - helping me to the car. Finally, I said, "This is so kind of you, but you don't have to do it every day. I enjoy your company, but if you have other things to do, I will understand.

"But you see," he said, "I need to do this every day." "Help me understand that," I answered.

"I need to do it for 2 reasons: I need to be sure that one of my favorite teachers is safe, and I need you to know that there is something more to me than being a gang leader."

I was able to tell him that I did feel safe with him around. Not because he was quite capable of walloping anyone that might try to hurt me, but because I had learned that his heart was becoming wise. Wisdom brings the long-term safety that violence cannot achieve. He thought a long time about that.

I was also able to tell him that I was very sure that he was many, many more things than a gang leader. I suggested that each day as we walk to the car, we explore the other things he is so that he can become those things more deeply.

Teaching and learning may begin in the classroom, but sometimes they continue in a parking lot. I decided that the best instructional strategy, in this case, for this student, was to park as far away as I could from the school entrance. We needed longer walks for all we had to discuss.

9. The Power of Love

by Shawna Smith

Shawna Smith currently teaches 2nd grade at Vale Elementary School in Cashmere, Washington.

It was my third year teaching, which for many teachers is the year that it all finally clicks. Struggles that once had been quite formidable seem a little bit easier. You're a veteran now, you know the ropes, and you've built somewhat of a reputation. The students and faculty know you and you have some credibility. Unfortunately, my third year was a huge transition year for me. I had just moved to a new town, a new house, a new school, and a new grade level. To top it off I was thrown into my job less than a week before school started. Bring on the stress!

The moment that first bell rang, and those beautiful children came flowing into my room, all my stress and nervous butterflies flew away and pure joy filled my heart. It was not going to be an easy year, however. I had heard stories from teachers that there are certain years where you get "that" bunch of kids, the group that tests your patience, make you rack your brain for new ideas, and make you really think if you're really cut out for this career. This was my year. I was given a classroom full of high energy and high needs, sweet children that needed all and everything I could possibly give.

One student in specific stuck out more than the others. Maybe it was the amount of times he had visited the principal, maybe it was fact that at second grade he was testing at a low kindergarten level, or maybe there was just something about him that made me want to dig deeper. This sweetie knew exactly how to push my every "teacher button", those emotional buttons we all have that cause our blood pressure to rise and our anger to simmer just below the surface. Motivation was not a word in his vocabulary and hard work was a foreign concept to him. A wise teacher once told me "more than discipline or structure, a child just needs to be loved". After the discipline and structure began to fail, I went straight to love.

My "love plan" was simple: whatever he did, however he acted, I made sure to find something good I could say to him. This wasn't always easy; sometimes I had to praise him for simply remembering to sit in his chair. At first, this child did not respond to the "love plan" the way I expected. He pushed back even more. He worked even less, which I did not know was even possible, and began stealing things from my classroom and other children's backpacks. Although his negative behavior increased, I simply continued to love him and praise him because it was my plan and I had decided to stick to it, and besides, I really had no other idea what to do at that point, (remember, this was only my third year of teaching.)

One day, I decided to pull this child back from P.E. and just have a chat with him. I knelt down and simply told him how much he meant to me. I told him that he was such an incredibly special person and how blessed I felt that he was in my class. I told him how smart he was and how I knew he could do so much better in class and on his work. I told him how excited I was for him and his future because he was made to do great things in life. What happened next is not what I ever expected. It's not in my teacher education books from college; it's not in any education manuals. If anything teachers are encouraged not to do this. I didn't intend it to happen. It just came out. I told him that I loved him.

I told him that I only wanted to make sure that he shines in any way that he can. I told him I believed in him and that he was special. At that very moment, all the walls that had been built up around this hard, disobedient, defiant child began to crumble. He flew into my arms and began to sob. As I held him in my arms I asked him what was wrong. His only response was "no one has ever said that to me before".

Instantly, I was overcome with emotion and tears flew down my cheeks. Here was a child, who, for eight years of his life, had never been told by anyone that he was loved. From that day on, that once headache of a child was nothing but sweet and obedient. His work ethic increased incredibly and by the end of the year he was working and testing at grade level. Although I am no longer his teacher, anytime he sees me he still runs my way for a great big hug and praise.

There are moments in teaching where the job seems incredibly overwhelming. Moments where the paycheck seems to disappear before it is even there, and you begin to question if this is what you're even supposed to do. However, there are also moments like this where every doubt and stress is completely erased and you are filled with confidence that there is nowhere else you're supposed to be. I have 180 days with these children to teach them, help them grow, and most importantly love them with every ounce of me. More than anything else, a child just needs to know that they are loved.

10. Choices

By Dr. Jim Uhlenkott

Jim Uhlenkott taught in the Mead School District for 18 years.

I lived, and still live, in the neighborhood where I taught. Many teachers have told me over the years that this was a mistake; it wasn't good to teach in your neighborhood school. They said the students can become too familiar; they know where you live and you can't have that needed separation between work and home. I never felt this way. My students did indeed know where I lived, as many of them lived in the same neighborhood and in two cases just two doors down in both directions. It was not uncommon to have students show up at my door with no real agenda other than to see what I was doing, or sometimes to ask if I could come out and ride bikes or go sledding with them. I enjoyed this and found it valuable.

Jesse was one of the kids in my neighborhood. I first met Jesse when he was in the first grade. I had seen him around the neighborhood, of course, and knew who he was at school, but had never actually met him or spent any time with him. I knew that Jesse was not a great student, at least not yet, but that he was a good kid. I also knew his temper could get away from him on occasion. It was one of these times that I first really met Jesse.

The elementary schools in our district did not have assistant principals, meaning that when the principal was out of the building for any reason the school could find itself with no real leader to handle difficult situations. To deal with this potential problem the school principals could appoint a "principal's designee": a teacher that would take over the principal position in their absence. I was that teacher. If our principal was out of the building for just a morning or an afternoon, I would stay in my classroom and just deal with the difficulties as they came up. A longer absence by the principal would mean I would have a substitute teacher take my class and I would spend the day (or two) in the office. My first meeting with Jesse was on one of these days.

The day was progressing smoothly with only the minor bumps in the road that are common to elementary schools. I spent most of my time in the office correcting student work while the substitute taught my class. This changed during lunch recess.

Mrs. Jones, Jesse's first grade teacher showed up at the office out of breath and clearly upset.

"He's gone," she said, "he's headed home. I don't know what he's upset about, but Jesse's headed home."

I looked out my window and saw Jesse walking across the playground to the woods. The woods separated our school from the neighborhood and most of the students used them as their normal route to and from school.

"Why's he upset?" I asked.

"Oh who knows? He always gets upset about something!" was her response.

I didn't have time to ask more questions then. Jesse was headed home and I knew that his mom worked during the day and no one would be there.

"Call his mom and tell her what is happening and that I'm going to bring him back to school," I yelled at the secretary, and I headed out the door. How exactly I was going to bring him back to school I didn't know yet.

"Jesse!" I called as I jogged across the playground. No response. His mind was clearly made up.

"Jesse, wait!"

Still no response. He was just about at the end of the playground and would be in the woods any moment. I took off in a run and caught up to him just as he entered the woods. I tried to place my hand on his shoulder but he shook it off and cursed at me.

"Leave me alone! Don't touch me!" These were his words minus the expletives.

I could not let him go home, so I grabbed him from behind in a sort of bear hug, knelt down and held him. He kicked and cried, yelling and cursing at me. I just held him until he finally got tired and relaxed a little.

"Jesse, you know who I am, don't you?"

"Yeah."

"I live right by you. We're neighbors," I said, trying to build a connection with him and also give him some time to calm down.

"Jesse, you have to come back to school with me."

The kicking and screaming started again, and again it subsided as he grew tired.

"Jesse, listen. There are two ways we can do this. I can pick you up, put you over my shoulder and carry you back. Everyone on the playground will see us. They'll see me carrying you and you crying and yelling, and they will all wonder, 'What's wrong with Jesse?' They'll talk about it all day, wondering what you did or what was wrong." I could tell he was thinking this through.

"Or," I said, "you and I can just walk back together. People will see us and think, 'There are Dr. U. and Jesse. I wonder what they are doing?' It will be just two friends walking across the playground together. Jesse, one of these things is going to happen. Which one do you want?"

He was much calmer at this point and he thought for a while.

"I'll walk back with you."

So we walked back and, as predicted, people noticed us but didn't really think much of it. I didn't have him come to the office right away. I wanted it to look as casual as possible and not that I had brought him to the office. I asked him if he'd come talk to me when recess was over. He did.

It turned out that Mrs. Jones had made an inappropriate comment to him. It made him mad, understandably so, and he took off. I agreed with him that her comment was indeed inappropriate and the three of us were able to work it out.

Jesse ended up in my classroom in sixth grade and was one of my favorite students ever. He was never a top student, and had great difficulties in reading and writing, but he was very bright and one of the best I've had at being able to see all sides of a problem. He was able to use this knowledge to synthesize information and evaluate situations, often finding the interconnections between seemingly unrelated concepts. This is somewhat rare in sixth grade students.

Like many poor readers, Jesse had been written off as "dumb" or "slow". Neither of these things was true. He just wasn't a good reader. If I could help him get the information he was just as capable as any other student, and better than most, at understanding it and engaging in higher-level thinking skills.

What made him one of my favorite students, however, was his unflinching honesty. If he was happy, you knew it. If he was hurt, you knew it. If he was angry, you knew it. If he appreciated you, you knew it. He rarely threw fits or lost his temper like he had in first grade, at least not in my class, but he also let you know exactly what he thought.

One day I was a little rushed and flustered as there were a lot of little "fires" to put out, and in this rushed and flustered state I responded curtly to Jesse's ask for help with a reading problem. He walked up to me, got in my face just a little and I could see the fire beginning to burn in his eyes. "I don't deserve that," he said, to which I replied, "You're right, Jesse. You don't. Forgive me." He did, and we went on as usual.

Three years later my family and I were driving in our mini-van downtown and were stopped at a traffic light. A young man was standing on the street corner, wearing dark clothing, and a long, black overcoat. He had black, spiked hair, multiple piercings on his face and many tattoos. We couldn't help but notice him as he approached cars, walking up to their window, tapping on them and saying something, perhaps asking for money. It was a little unnerving and my wife, our four children and I were all hoping the light would change and we could move on before he got to us.

It didn't. He reached the car in front of us, tapped on the window, said something, and evidently got no response. He stood up, looked at us, and then came walking quickly to our van. His pace quickened as he got closer, and then this kid smiled, ran up to our van, and pounded with his hands on my window. I was looking for any escape route from this kid when all of a sudden I hear him yell, "Dr. U! Dr. U!" It was Jesse. I quickly rolled down my window and reached out to grab his hand. We couldn't talk long as the light had changed, but our exchange was meaningful and heartfelt. It was Jesse; one of my favorite students ever.

11. A Day in the Life

By Bob Isitt

Bob Isitt taught and coached for 37 years at the junior and high school level in Spokane, Washington.

Real Life

It is pretty easy to think that teaching our students is all about lesson plans, effective assessment, classroom management techniques and the other issues that are printed in textbooks and show up in reports and teacher evaluations. It would be nice if it were that simple. Our students, however, live in worlds outside of our classrooms, and these worlds impact the lives of our students more than we can imagine.

My first teaching position was at a poverty-area junior high school. I was also the track coach there and tried to get as many of my students as I could to turn out for track. I knew that many of my students had difficult home lives and I believed that an after-school program could provide the relationships and camaraderie that students of that age need.

One day a boy, a great kid, was a bit lethargic so I asked him what was going on. He said his dad's smoking really got to him last night. I asked why it would bother him during the night. His answer: My dad has the bottom bunk.

Another one of my athletes could not perform one day because he was in a lot of pain. Had bruises up and down his body. When I asked him what was going on he said his mom's boyfriend whupped him. What struck me is not so much the beating, as horrible as that was, but how nonchalant he was about it. Sadly, that was his life and he really didn't see it being unusual. This was his life and he accepted it as normal.

These are just two examples of what happens in the lives of our students every day. Some have it much worse. It's hard to expect them to focus on math, social studies and their other courses when they go home every night to very difficult situations.

There are also, however, many moments that make you smile, and for very different reasons.

Tough Requirements!

I was sitting in the coaches' locker room listening to the frosh football coach explain to one of his athletes that he was "ineligible" to play because he was failing Math. The boy's response was, "I can't play football just because I'm in 'algebra'!!??"

Didn't you use to be somebody?

In my later years of teaching high school I started to think that it might be time to retire when twin senior girls in my class came up to me in the hallway and asked if I had ever taught at a certain junior high school. I told them that, yes, I did teach at that school, and then I waited for them to tell me how I had taught someone they knew and that I was their favorite teacher. Instead, they looked at me with very puzzled expressions. One of them said their mom had me when she was in the 8th grade. I said that was very possible and waited for the response I was sure was coming. They again started staring at me with a most quizzical look on their faces as if they didn't believe their mom. Finally one of them asks me, "Did you USE to be good looking?"

Showing up for Class.

In my junior class of American Government, I would have a lot of discussion and debates over issues rather than having my students simply memorize all the committees and duties etc. The class was interrupted one day when I was asked to send a certain boy to the office. On his way out I asked what was going on. He said he's getting suspended for not going to his classes. I was surprised when he said this because he rarely missed my class. So I asked him why he came to my class and not the others. His answer was that he loved the discussions and debates. Thinking and truly discussing alternative ideas gets people involved, adults as well as junior high students. Learning becomes more enjoyable, more effective and productive. All of our students are capable and want to learn. It's our job to give them an outlet for their thoughts and opinions.

Oops!

One year while teaching high school, I had the son of a state legislator who had a reputation for being extremely hot headed and aggressive. I caught his son cheating one day and it just so happened we were going to have Open House that evening, so I thought I should let the dad know about his boy's fall from the straight and narrow. I got a big chewing out and was forcefully informed that HIS son would NEVER do anything like that. Bodily harm was not so farfetched. Later that evening I went through the papers the students had turned in so I could show this man proof of his son's cheating ways. Well, it turned out I had mixed up students. His son hadn't cheated and had actually done quite well! I contacted the boy's father and apologized for my mistake. Thankfully he was kind enough to forgive me. Whew!!

12. What Really Matters

By Holly Myers

Holly Myers was a first grade teacher at Dorothy Fox Elementary School in Camas, Washington.

My teaching career began in the typical fashion. I took the required teacher education courses, completed my student teaching, received my degree and teaching certificate and then went out into the work force. Like all teachers, I had a philosophy of education that was born out of my years as a student as well as the information and skills I learned in college, but this philosophy changed dramatically the year Matthew came into my life.

I had been a first grade teacher for several years and classroom management had come fairly easy for me. I was good at relating effectively to individual students and maintaining structure in the semi chaotic environment that is typical in first grade classrooms. Matthew, however, wasn't a typical first grader. I had never seen such a young child create so much commotion in a classroom.

My education from him started on his first day of school. I had given the normal classroom talk laying out clear rules and expectations to help the kids get adjusted. I wanted them to know this was my classroom and that I expected proper behavior. I spelled out simple but clear rules and guidelines just as I had every year.

Matthew came from a single parent home with a mom with mental health issues. His kindergarten year had not gone well, so Matthew had moved in with his father and stepmother. Matthew was not lacking in any mental health areas, but had never been given much oversight.   He had run the home for years. Kindergarten had been a disaster because his mom had allowed him to stay home any time he didn't want to come to school. The days he did show up all classroom order disappeared. He was the kind of kid that pulled everyone off task and challenged every rule. He was also extremely bright and darling to look at which wasn't always helpful.

During that first day of school, I had many talks with Matthew about not climbing on top of the desk to dance or yelling out at any random moment.   He constantly drew attention to himself which directed all the other children away from anything I was trying to accomplish. Things had escalated so badly one day that I got down on my knees in front of him and said, "You may think you can do what you want, but this is my classroom and I am in charge. You need to follow the rules and this is not negotiable with me."

These talks caused a slight bit of behavior change but not enough. I constantly needed to correct, redirect and have little "talks" with Matthew, taking time and attention off all my other students.

On the third day of the year he was kicked off the playground for his unruly behavior. When it was time for the class to go to outside, I put him at the end of the line so that I could take him to the principal's office where he was to spend his recess time. There were a few turns in the hallway and I couldn't always see my entire line of students. By the time we reached the outside door I realized Matthew was not with us anymore. I let the class outside and went looking for him.

I quickly retraced my steps back down the hallway and saw my teaching partner coming towards me with Matthew in tow. "Matthew decided to water the bathroom," she said.

She had heard something spraying on the walls as she passed the bathroom. The door had been left open and he had been caught in the act of urinating all over the walls.

I took him to the principal's office, where he was talked to about not being respectable and that there would be a punishment for his actions. This was during the time that spankings, with parent consent, were a commonly-delivered consequence for certain kinds of problem. The stepmom supported the need for him to learn about having boundaries and was okay with this punishment. He was given one easy swat. He was also required to clean the bathroom and I was very meticulous about him doing it well. It took him forty-five minutes to finish the task.

I felt horrible that his first week of school had been so negative. Monday morning I called him in from the playground before school started. We sat down and had a little talk. I started out saying that I really cared about him and that last week must have been very rough. I told him that I had some ideas that could help this week go better.

I let him know that I thought he was a very smart boy and that we all wanted to find ways to help him do well at our school. I wanted him to know that we can work it out together.

"When you don't know what to do or don't understand something, I can help you. If we work together this can be a very good year for you!"

That day was different. His behavior was much better. I didn't know if it was from our talk or the strong reprimand he had been given at the end of the previous week but things were definitely improving. I still had to have many little talks and reminders with Matthew. He still wanted to be the center of attention and to run the show, but things were better. He had no skills at all for first grade so he needed a lot of extra time and help, but by the end of the year he was doing very well.

The biggest change, however, was in me. I began the year by telling Matthew that this was my classroom and that he would do things my way or else. As the year went on it became our classroom. Matthew was invested in the things we were doing because he had a say in them. We were working together.

Many, perhaps most of us, don't like to be ruled by a dictator. We want our voice to be heard; we want our opinions to be considered. We want to matter to someone. Matthew mattered. He was a smart boy with good ideas. I began to matter to Matthew when he believed he mattered to me.

I liked this boy. He needed boundaries, but also needed to know people really cared about him. During that year he would always sit next to me and give me little secret hugs before he left each day. Years later I learned when he was graduating from high school that I was his favorite teacher.

I had thought that order and good classroom management were the most important part of teaching until Matthew helped me learn this lesson: students need to know that you care about them more than anything else. Building relationships with students is the bond that truly holds the classroom together. Students will invest in the goals you set before them after you have invested in them as people.

I never saw him Matthew again, but he changed how I ran my classrooms from that day forward. Students need to know I care about them first.

13. Me? A Teacher?

By Ashlyn Mundo

Ashlyn Mundo is now a literacy instructor at Chief Leschi Schools in Puyallup, Washington.

I am currently a student teaching candidate, and the end of my educator preparation program is fast approaching. The last few moments of my long journey I am given to reflection, going back to the beginning, the spur in the direction that time and actions has now led me. My journey to become a teacher and to pursue the calling of facilitating the dreams and achievements among young minds all comes back to one moment in time and one individual in my past. A teacher. For the sake of this individual's confidentiality, I will refer to this teacher as Ms. Johnson.

It was the first time I had ever stepped foot as a student into a traditional school building. My stomach ached with emptiness as I was not able to eat earlier that morning. I felt a cold sweat form on my forehead, drops of uncertainty, and my head was spinning. I was nervous. Right next to me was my best friend since third grade, but I still felt completely vulnerable and uncomfortable in this new environment. I had done my back-to-school shopping with my mom, packed everything I might need, and even had a brand new outfit on, one that made me appear like the high schooler I now was. It seemed as if nothing could ease my apprehension. The building seemed giant, the hallways ominous, and my locker, nearly impossible to open.

This was the first day of my freshman year in high school. I was a new kid, just like the other 380 incoming freshman. However, this was also my first day of public school, or for that matter a traditional classroom school of any kind. I was homeschooled from pre-school until eighth grade, and had spent the last nine years of my education with one teacher, a constantly changing and moving classroom, and no distractors during my learning. My parents often would take my brother and me traveling, and somehow manage to implement studies into our destinations. During our road trip through Chehalis, Washington, we took notes at the Lewis and Clark Museum for a report that we would write up upon our return. On our long family vacations in

Hawaii, we would go to the nearby aquarium to observe marine life, and connect it to what we had been studying about ecosystems. Also, at home, we would go to parks, the library, or simply work at our dining table for our lessons. I knew learning as a process with no boundaries.

I was not the awkward, socially out-of-tune homeschooler that is sometimes stereotyped. I played sports for years up until this point of my life. I got along with the athletes. We would travel throughout our state and often to other states, such as Colorado, California, Oregon, Texas, and Florida for competitive tournaments. On these trips, I grew close with my teammates, and as a result, I was able to befriend athletes, not all of whom were academically focused. I even had played fast pitch softball at the local middle school, so I knew many students who were starting at my high school, too. However, my comfort level on the field and with my teammates did not translate to an ability to become comfortable in this new place, with procedures that were foreign to me, and around people that were unfamiliar to me.

Looking back, this transition was actually relatively easy. I was more than prepared for the content in my classes, my work ethic built from years of independent homeschooling was far beyond most of my peers, and I had more friends at the school than I had first thought. However, despite how easy the transition may seem now, I remember how incredibly terrifying it was for my fourteen year-old self to embark upon. I actually lost weight from losing my appetite at school due to the heightened nervousness I was now feeling. It also did not help that I have always been an exceedingly shy person. As a young child, I hid behind my mother's leg. As an elementary aged student, I had to be coaxed to stay in the children's service at church with my peers and away from my parents. Also, as an adolescent, I rarely knew how to begin conversations, and merely waited for them to come to me. I was told by one of my friends later, as we neared graduation, that he was unsure if I ever spoke during freshman year. It was that extreme.

I remember going from one classroom to the next on this first day of my public school life, all of it somewhat of a blur. First period, the girl next to me talked a little bit; that was nice. I cannot recall second period, what class it was, who taught it, or what my first day was like. Actually, my recollection of third, fourth, and sixth periods are similarly non-descript and uneventful. The only reason why I remember my first period is because that was my first period of public schooling. It was the first time I sat in an assigned seat. It was the first time I waited for the attendance call. It was also the day that I met my current best friend. It would take almost a year, but eventually that girl who talked to me and sat next to me on my first day in my first period would have a few group projects with me, she would invite me over to play neighborhood touch football, we would become friends, and still drive to each other's college campuses to spend some quality friend time. There was one other memorable class period that first day, however: fifth period, my Honors English-Language Arts class.

Up until this point in the day I had been doing well navigating the crowded halls, but for some reason I struggled trying to find my fifth period class, and was running up against the bell. I did not know exactly what the consequences were for not being in the classroom when the bell rang, but I figured they could not be desirable, so naturally, I began to panic. In my rush, I hustled right past Ms. Johnson as she was standing in the doorway of her classroom, greeting her students as they came to her room. My panic increased as it became obvious that I had no idea where my next class might be, so I rushed back to this teacher and asked her if she could tell me where this classroom and teacher were located. I was a little surprised, embarrassed and relieved when she smiled at me and told me that I was in the right place after all; she was my next teacher and this was my classroom! My embarrassment subsided as Ms. Johnson handled my awkward situation with such grace and warmth, and none of the other students had noticed, so I felt golden.

Now, why does this all matter? Even though this day's description may seem very routine and ordinary, it is something that has had the sticking power in my memory for over seven years, and is not something that I will soon forget. I remember the instant comfort that I felt walking into Ms. Johnson's classroom. She had decorated it with posters of flowers and other spring-type decorations. It was nothing out of the ordinary. The true secret lay within the way she interacted with my peers and with me. She treated us with respect. She was young, not fresh out of college, but young enough to be able to relate to her students, to reach us on our level. She could speak our language. We were fourteen or fifteen-year old teenagers who were glued to their cellphones and had an established a language from the ever popular text messaging. Ms. Johnson would communicate occasionally using expressions that we used, yet still modeled the necessary proper

English grammar and syntax that is essential of an English teacher. She would toss out words, such as *chillax*, *tricked out*, or *swag* in appropriate situations, but whenever delivering instruction where we were expected to model her way of speaking, she would use a much higher-level of English.

Ms. Johnson treated each one of us with respect and undeniable care. She was constantly checking up on us in class about our grades, or assignments we had missed. She approached students who were purposely refusing to turn in work by putting their needs first, meaning that she phrased her addresses, with "I am concerned for you…" As simple as this may seem, it meant the world to students such as me, who were looking for people in this new unfamiliar world who truly cared about us as an individuals. She knew my name within the first week, and in this strange new world of high school, when it felt like I was getting lost in the crowd, she showed me that I was worth remembering. This notion was not one that I had the privilege of having in abundance in the first few months of my high school experience.

Ms. Johnson's caring nature toward her students did not simply stop at the personable level, but also showed in her investment and devotion to her job as an educator. I always noticed her at school when I got there early, and she was also there whenever I needed to stay late. She would spend hours grading, and truly scrutinizing our writing samples, making meaningful comments which she expected that we implement before their return. She was available for additional instruction anytime it seemed that I needed it. I remember her taking her lunch time to help me perfect an upcoming essay, which was passing already; in fact, it was probably a solid "B". Looking back I feel bad for taking her time on such a miniscule problem. I was that student who strove for all A's. Nevertheless, Ms. Johnson was willing to work with me to improve my writing to the next level. I was not in any danger of failing either her class or the WASL (Washington Assessment of Student Learning, the standardized test of Washington at the time of my graduation). I was not the student that needed extra support to reach a standard level or even an accomplished level. I simply wanted to strive to do my best, and Ms. Johnson was willing to put in her end of the effort in order for me to reach an exemplary level.

I admired her, because her work ethic was one that I was comfortable modeling. Unlike many of my other teachers who chose to do only what was required, Ms. Johnson made her classroom an area of excellence and hard work, which stemmed from her own work and instruction. I remember feeling a sense of obligation to avoid putting in minimal effort to get the desired grade, but always put forth my best work, because that is what Ms. Johnson did for us. Long before I ever considered becoming a teacher, I admired the way she ran her classroom. I enjoyed her class, which successfully made me fall in love with writing both creatively and academically.

Three years after I had passed Ms. Johnson's class with a 4.0, I met up with her just weeks before graduation. Now, as a well-established senior in high school, I had new issues to sort out, one of which was a major for college. She referred back to my excellent work in her class in both writing and analytical reading. She also recalled the way I was able to assist my peers when they needed help, and how much she had appreciated it at the time. I was completely unaware of this contribution then, but when I thought back to it, I did recall reiterating and re-explaining some concepts to my peers who were slower to understand the material. Next, in our conversation, Ms. Johnson asked me if I had ever considered teaching. Shocked, I told her that I had not. I had considered marine biology, physical training, and sports medicine, but never teaching.

"Well, you seem to have natural talent," Ms. Johnson had told me. "Plus, you are always such a caring and hardworking individual. Students would be lucky to have you as a teacher."

Despite her encouraging words, I did not come to any kind of a conclusion during our little conversation, but her words were burned in my memory. She was the first one who addressed my future abilities as a teacher, and had believed in me at a time where I was about to enter into a whole new realm of uncertainty. Ms. Johnson's words carried extra weight because of my respect for her and when it came time to decide on a major in college, her comment echoed throughout my thoughts.

The time came for me to submit my green form to declare my major. As I prepared to do so I had a flashback to that conversation with Ms. Johnson and the genuine smile she had on her face when she addressed my future. I never would have thought that one, non-related individual could make such a difference. I especially never would have expected that that fearful first day of high school would be the beginning to such an amazing journey. Yes, Ms. Johnson's words during that casual conversation carried a significant amount of weight and influence, but in the end, it was her actions that impacted me the most. I have frequently thought back to her throughout my teacher preparation program, to the way she had handled particular situations, or how she approached certain topics. I try to model her enthusiasm and her work ethic in everything that I do in the classroom. Truly, Ms. Johnson's words encouraged me, her instruction changed me, and her actions and caring nature inspired me.

14. Just a Little Nudge

By Don Kardong

Don Kardong taught sixth grade for three years in Spokane, Washington.

Like many classroom teachers, I read to the students almost every day after recess, both to settle them down and, hopefully, get them interested in reading for fun. One spring I decided to read them The Hobbit, a book I had read myself and that I thought would be especially entertaining for my class. After a few weeks, though, I sensed that a lot of the students weren't really connecting with the story, so I asked for a show of hands of those who wanted me to continue and those who didn't. It was close, but it looked like almost half the class wanted me to read something else.

"I don't want to continue reading this if so many of you aren't enjoying it," I told them. "But if you want to finish it on your own, you can find the book in the school library."

A few minutes later, as we were shuffling around to get ready for afternoon subjects, a student named Benny came up to my desk.

"Mr. Kardong," he said, "I like that story about hobbits and things."

"That's great," I answered. "You should check out the book from the library."

Benny was a wonderful kid, but a pretty average sixth grade student. I was glad he had enjoyed the story, but I didn't have high hopes for him checking out the book and finishing it. He didn't mention The Hobbit again that spring, and I pretty much forgot about our discussion as the school year wound down and the class graduated from elementary school and moved on to junior high.

A few weeks into the next fall, a woman who I could not immediately identify walked into my classroom. I want to say she came stomping in, but that's a little unfair. Let's just say she entered with an air of authority, someone with something important to relate. I held my breath, wondering if this was the mother of someone I had supposedly wronged in some way. That did happen now and then.

"Mr. Kardong," she said when she reached my desk, "I'm Benny's mother, and I just want to thank you for what you did for him."

I had no idea what she was talking about, so I asked.

"He went to the library and got that book you were reading last spring," she explained. "After he finished it, he read those other three big books."

She meant the Lord of the Rings trilogy. Frankly, I'd never known anyone Benny's age who had read them all.

"Now he's reading all kinds of books," she continued, "And his grades are all improving. I've been told by other teachers that eventually Benny would find someone who would get him excited about reading. Thank you so much for doing that."

You never know the impact you may be having, right? You never know what may or may not sink in or ignite a spark of interest. I certainly was never convinced that I was turning Benny or any other student on to reading by reading to them, even though that was the point, but there it was, a victory in the trenches.

As luck would have it, I saw Benny a few months later. "Benny," I said, "your mom says you read the Lord of the Rings trilogy."

"Yes," he answered. "Have you read them?"

"Yes," I responded. "Twice."

"So have I," said Benny. He wasn't bragging, by the way, just reporting.

A few years after that, I was boarding a plane and I recognized Benny and said hello. He said hello back, then buried his nose back in the book he was reading. It was something other than Lord of the Rings.

15. Showing Human

By Dr. Doreen Keller

Dr. Doreen Keller is a professor of education at Whitworth University in Spokane, Washington.

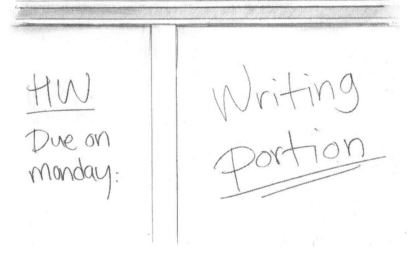

The clock had stopped. Literally stopped. Every once in a while the electronic system that governed the wall clocks in the building needed to be reset or recalibrated or re-something to official district time, and when it happened, the paper-thin red second hand stood still.

It did this to torment the 28 students in our sixth-period sophomore English class in an unusually sadistic way this day. The long scarlet line stood poised on the number twelve while the thick black arms told us it was 2:25, five minutes shy of the end of the school day. None of us knew how long it would remain 2:25 on this unseasonably warm Monday in March that marked (maybe for the first time in history of school athletics) a pleasant, sunny beginning to the spring sports season in Spokane, Washington.

I didn't notice the clock at first as I was trying to squeeze in as much preparation with my students as possible before they sat down in a week's time to finally face the writing portion of their high-stakes state assessment. Until, that is, Mike Merten started twitching more than usual. This fifteen-year-old boy was the prototypical kinesthetic learner. I used all the tricks from my classroom management tool box for this end-of-the-day, mostly-boy class, and Mr. Merten was my biggest challenge and prize - if I had him, I had them all. I would ask him to be my helper; he would lead our Latin root actions, and he was always up to the task of finding some good music when our work called for it. I made sure we transitioned into manageable chunks of varied activities, but for some reason on this warm March afternoon, he was unreachable.

I had always appreciated Mr. Merten's energy and even as a newer teacher I was able to enjoy the organized chaos that sometimes ensued, but today was different. I was genuinely worried about some of them and their performance on the upcoming test. They had been pretty darn engaged and intent on improving as the test week approached, but not now, not at this perpetually 2:25 moment. I noticed Mike staring at the clock, and looked to see that everyone else was, too. Then I saw what had them in such a tizzy. The stoppage was wreaking havoc on their adolescent bodies and souls. I tried to ignore, to go on. No success. Avoidance wasn't going to make this one go away, and that red line still wasn't moving. I gave up and stared right along with them.

Finally, Becca asked, "Mrs. Keller, what's wrong?"

"Well, Becca," I replied, "We are all ready to get outside today, aren't we?"

"I suppose so," she answered back as she closed her binder.

I looked at Mr. Merten and saw something in his eye. Was it a tear? What was going on here? Then, magically, the second hand start moving again, and Mike couldn't hold back any longer.

He shot up out of his seat and ripped his pants off. Yes, his pants. Off. He did this with pizazz the way NBA stars shed their warm-ups when they are game ready. In one dramatic, solid, fluid motion he tore his sweat pants from his legs, gave them a couple bold swirls over his head, and then threw them to the back of the room. Beneath those pants were his yet-to-be-broken-in, midnight-blue, silky Adidas soccer shorts.

I cried. I couldn't talk. I was laughing so hard my stomach ached. And the entire class was right there with me. We were all sharing a moment we would remember for years. And they loved to see me let go, enjoy, relax and not know what to do. I told them to go and have a ball in the sun.

This memory of my classroom on that hot afternoon with students I thoroughly enjoyed, no, loved, has held significance for years. It informs how I approach teaching today. Earlier in my teaching career I struggled to be more emotionally available with my students. I thought in my first couple years that if I were over-prepared, fair, organized, and excited about my subject matter, then the kids would learn. And despite my relational inaccessibility to them during these years, some of them did learn. But this and a few other events like it taught me a great deal. After our Mike Merten spring sports kick-off striptease, our class changed a bit—students walked in the room with broader smiles on their faces. As long as I offered some authentic glimpses of letting go and spending time with them for the sake of getting to know and celebrate them as humans, our other more serious times were full of engagement and being intentional in our pursuit of the learning targets.

Informed by this and other experiences like it, I now think teaching is first and foremost a craft of relating to other humans. Our students can be seven years old, 15 years old, or 20 years old; they are all humans. At the beginning of my career I took for granted that since my students were physically present they would want to learn in our classroom; otherwise, why would they be there? What I found over time was that if they knew me in a human way—some of my interests, my life outside school, my history—and if I took time to know them in this way, the sky was the limit for things we could try inside and outside the room. I could transform from this talking bubble at the front of the room to someone who was a human and had feelings and passions. I could transform into someone who they knew cared about them.

When I would facilitate novel, creative classroom experiences for them before this relational piece was my focus, I would come up against resistance, sometimes even a lack of trust. After living in a place where we both saw each other as humans, not them just seeing me as a teacher, and I just seeing them as students, I could propose just about anything—a walk out to a cold, dark baseball shed on a winter afternoon to make a scene from the novel Night come alive, a sword battle in the middle of our school courtyard using words instead of swords to make Shakespearian language a little less intimidating.

Some teachers have this relational piece down without having to think about it. Other teachers never figure out that it is the most important and delicate balance that takes place between teacher and student. I know now, in my 15th year of teaching, this piece of showing human must take priority before any authentic, experiential learning can take place.

16. The Reluctant Learner

By Dr. Patricia Luse

Dr. Luse is a former elementary teacher and a retired professor of education at Eastern Washington University.

By the time I met Dr. Hee I had been teaching for at least fifteen years. I had been in two different school districts and had worked for five different principals. I was a competent teacher, had received praise from both students and parents, and had been nominated for Teacher of the Year. There wasn't much that I felt I couldn't do in the realm of the elementary classroom.

From the first introduction, there was something about Dr. Hee that just did not sit too well with me. She was intelligent, had several years of teaching experience behind her and had been hired to fill the position of Gifted and Talented Coordinator. This was a gaping hole in the school curriculum that had been previously covered by providing one day a week of release time for one of the classroom teachers. The teacher who worked in the position was very confident and provided excellent guidance to the students, but did not have the time to devote the necessary energy to build a strong and comprehensive program to meet the diverse needs of the gifted student population. Dr. Hee would work in the coordinator position on a full-time basis, and thus be able to develop the desired comprehensive program. So, it wasn't Dr. Hee's qualifications that bothered me; it was her aggressive and commanding way of presenting her ideas.

Dr. Hee decided to change the pullout program that had been the model used for many years, to an in-class program. The students' individual differences would be met by providing various ways for the students to demonstrate what they had learned about a particular subject area. These activities would take the form of differentiated activities developed by the teacher and offered to the students for their selection. These changes were announced at a faculty meeting, and all teachers were required to attend five after-school in-service sessions to learn how to adapt student requirements to differentiated choices.

I resisted strongly from the very first session of in-service, as I sat in the back of the room, corrected papers, and occasionally looked up at Dr. Hee who was explaining the philosophy behind the differentiated activities. I did not have any problem with Dr. Hee's ideas, but my lessons were already excellent ones and my students learned and demonstrated their knowledge in very innovative ways. I did not see why I had to change; after all I was an excellent teacher. There were many other teachers in the building that needed this workshop, but my teaching was just fine the way it was. I had worked hard to develop the diorama assignment for the Native Americans study, the overhead transparency assignment for the health unit, and the filmstrip assignment for the weather unit. These were already very challenging and different ways for the students to display their knowledge. And so, I sat in the back of the room and glowered, muttering to myself that even though I was in the in-service, no one could make me change what I was doing in my own classroom.

However, I was wrong. The principal calmly informed me that Dr. Hee would be working with me in my classroom to implement the use of differentiated activities in my Native Americans unit of study. I protested that I did not need Dr. Hee's help, I could manage on my own and I would rather work by myself. My protests fell on deaf ears and two weeks later Dr. Hee showed up at my classroom door, all smiles, ready to help me implement something that I saw no need for.

Jody was an average fifth grade student, very well behaved with an out-going personality. He was well-liked, had many friends, and never failed to offer help whenever the need arose in the classroom. Jody's dedication to his schoolwork involved putting forth just enough energy to meet the minimum requirements of assignments. The quality of his work was adequate, but it was nothing that would win any awards. So, it was with amazement that after three weeks of exposure to all of Dr. Hee's ideas, I heard Jody tell Dr. Hee that he would like to do a skit for his final project for the unit on Native Americans.

"A skit!" I thought. "Why, Jody barely completes the required assignments, whatever will he do if he has to plan, write, and design a skit all by himself?"

I listened with skepticism as Dr. Hee and Jody discussed some initial ideas for his skit.

Project day arrived and students entered the classroom carrying posters, plaster models, and bags filled with who-knows-what. I watched for Jody and saw him come into the room empty-handed. I nodded to myself that Jody would prove me right about the idea of offering differentiated activities as choices!

When it was Jody's turn to present his skit, he said he needed to go into the hall and get ready. He disappeared and the class waited. One minute passed, then two, I was just getting ready to go look for him when the door opened. Into the room paddled Jody.

He had constructed a cardboard canoe that hung from his shoulders by leather straps. Jody used a cardboard paddle and circled the classroom describing the trees covered with hanging moss that lined the banks of the river. He explained how his tribe used native plants for food and medicine. He pointed out the birds and wildlife he saw from his canoe, and then he took a bow and arrow from the quiver on his back, and calmly shot a deer. He then explained to the class how he used the skin of the deer to make clothing and moccasins, the sinew to sew the clothing and the meat of the animal for food.

The students and I were spellbound. We could see what Jody was describing just as easily as if we had been in an Eastern Woodlands swamp. My heart swelled with pride for Jody and his outstanding presentation; and at the same time, my heart was filled with shame for almost denying this opportunity for Jody to shine.

This humbling experience with Dr. Hee and Jody took place over ten years ago but I share it with my teacher-education students to illustrate the value and effectiveness of allowing students the option of choice. Had I not been forced to work with Dr. Hee and give my students the option of choosing how they wished to present their knowledge, I would still think of Jody today as just an average, well-liked student. I would not be aware of Jody's thirst for knowledge or his unique way of demonstrating that knowledge to the class.

I am grateful to my principal for forcing me to work with Dr. Hee, for her ideas and for opening my eyes to the value of giving choice to my students, and I am grateful that I had the opportunity to learn from Jody. He taught me a great deal about education, learning, and choices – and he illustrated very clearly if you offer students choices you may be giving them the keys to unlock wonderful, hidden talents.

17. The Phone Call

By Dr. Jim Uhlenkott

Jim Uhlenkott taught in the Mead School District for 18 years.

This was not the job I wanted. My course work in college, all of my classroom observations and my student teaching had all been at the elementary level. I reminded myself of this fact as I walked up the steps of my first place of employment as a teacher: Mead Jr. High School.

I was hired for this job because I was a literacy major in college, a new field of study at the time, and Mead Jr. High needed a reading specialist for their struggling students. I had been hoping for an elementary position, but this was a job in a great district and teaching jobs were hard to come by even then.

The vice-principal pulled no punches in the interview.

"These are 8th and 9th graders with serious reading problems," he told me (the junior high school was 8th and 9th grade in this district at the time), "and when you are that old and can't read you often have others serious issues as well. You'll have small class sizes with large class problems."

This was not exactly the uplifting talk I was hoping for, but I appreciated his honesty.

He was right. My classes were small, the smallest had six students and the largest was only thirteen, but almost every student had other factors, serious ones that they brought to class with them. Drug abuse was common, as were poor living conditions, difficult home lives and anxiety and depression disorders.

One of my first and most important jobs was just getting my students to work with me as I attempted to help them become better readers. It took time for them to trust me and to believe that I could actually help them. The first semester began slowly, but then I gained their trust and by the end of that semester many of these young people had made significant gains in reading. It was a tough job, but I was enjoying it.

The semester was coming to a close and I walked from my classroom to the office after 6th period had ended. The students were all walking out to the buses to go home, with the loud and boisterous enthusiasm that comes with being in junior high. I went to check the mail in my box and looked it over as I watched the students going through the hallway through the large windows of the school office. Not much in my mail was very interesting that day, except for the class rosters for the upcoming semester. I happen to look up from the list of next semester's class lists and saw a particular student passing by the office window. I knew him by reputation. We all knew him by reputation. I'll call him Tom Smith.

Tom Smith was huge for a junior high student, easily 5'11" and ripped. He was a 15, almost 16 year old ninth grader and a terror at our school. He was always in trouble, serious trouble. The police had been to our school on multiple occasions just to see him. He seemed to enjoy hurting people. We had entire faculty meetings where the only topic was how to deal with Tom. As I looked up from my papers he happened to look my direction and our eyes locked, and he gave me the glare: the "Tom glare" we called it, and it scared you, right down to your toes. I froze. His eyes continued to bore into mine as he walked down the hall, and just before he was to pass out of sight, he flipped me off.

I did not know what to do. The typical teacher move at this point would be to go out in the hall, chase him down and discipline him for the rude gesture. Discipline him? How? He was younger, stronger and faster than me and he enjoyed hurting people. I didn't move, deciding discretion, in this case, was the better part of valor.

I took a breath, and once again turned my attention to the class roster for the next semester.

Glancing down the list of students for each period I saw a lot of now-familiar names. It was exciting to see the students I would have again as well as the new ones I would meet and I read over each period's list with a certain sense of anticipation – until I got to period 6. There, toward the bottom of the list, on my class roster was the name I hoped I'd never see.

Tom Smith. In my class. Sixth period. Great! I don't even know the guy and he already hates me! I might get beat up on the first day!

The new semester arrived and the first day was fairly easy and followed a predictable routine. I told the students about myself to begin building a relationship with them, talked about the class and what we would be doing and gave them a pep talk about how I could help them with their reading. I could, if they worked with me, help them become better readers and be more successful not only in school but in life. I asked each student to fill out a form telling me about their interests and hobbies so I could help them find a book they might enjoy reading. This usually went well and the periods passed by quickly.

Each period the students came in the room, as you would expect in a junior high school. They were a little loud with some minor pushing and shoving and I'd have to work just a bit to quiet them down so I could begin. This was true the whole day, with the exception of period 6.

The students of sixth period came in quietly, almost solemnly, barely speaking at all. They all knew Tom was in this class and no one wanted to be the one to set him off. They came in, sat down, and looked straight ahead. Tom came in last. He walked in slowly, went to the back of the room, sat down and put his feet on the back of the desk in front of him, and looked straight at me. Apparently it was my time to begin.

Okay. I took a breath and started talking. I went through my same routine, handed out the forms, collected them, and the period ended. The students got up and handed me the forms as they filed out of the room and headed for the buses to go home. Tom handed me his form as well. I expected it to be blank, or full of expletives, but it wasn't. Not only had he filled it out just like everyone else, his actually had more detail on it than some. I was truly surprised. This day was a great success! No blood! No one got hurt, and Tom did as I asked! This was more than I had hoped for.

Suddenly I got an idea. I don't know where it came from or why I did it, but I did. I quickly went into the office, grabbed a phone and called Tom's dad. I had no idea if he would be home. From the stories I heard he wasn't home often. To my surprise he answered the phone. The conversation went like this:

Hello?

Mr. Smith? This is Mr. Uhlenkott at the junior high school. I'm Tom's special reading teacher.

A short pause.

What'd he do now?

Another pause. I wasn't expecting this.

Well Mr. Smith, Tom has not done anything wrong. In fact, today was the first day of the new semester and I wanted to let you know that Tom did very well in class. I think he's going to have a very good semester.

Another pause. Was he still on the line?

Ok. Thanks. 'click'

And he hung up.

I wasn't sure if that was a successful phone call or not. Oh well, I tried.

The next day the classes went well as I began to work with my students in each period. I could work with them individually due to the small class sizes and I was given a full-time aide to assist me. There were no real surprises, until sixth period. I wondered how the period would go and was hoping that Tom would once again be willing to comply and do some work with me. "Some" was all I was hoping for. I couldn't have been more wrong.

Tom came in sixth period smiling and happy. He slapped me on the shoulder (man, he was strong!) said "Hey, Mr. U," and sat in his seat in the back of the room. I tried not to look too shocked and we started to work. Tom not only did everything I asked, he did it with real effort. He was pleasant, treated others well and worked hard. I wondered how long this would last. Would this "honeymoon" period end? Would something happen to set him off and we'd see the "old" Tom again? Something did.

I had structured my class to accommodate the students' short attention spans. We worked for 20 minutes, took a 10 minute break where we would talk or I would let them challenge me at "hangman", and then we would work the last 20 minutes. If the class got a little loud while they were working, as is typical in a junior high school, I'd say something like, "Okay, quiet down or you'll lose your break." This usually sufficed and things would settle down.

One day the students again got a little loud so I said my line fully expecting that would be the end of it.

"Okay, settle down so you don't lose your break."

In the back of the room, Tom looked up from his work. He had that glare again, the "Tom glare", the one I saw that day as he passed me in the hall. Everyone went silent. Tom slowly stood up, his chair scraping menacingly against the linoleum floor. It was like a scene from the classic movie "High Noon" where all you hear is your heartbeat and the tick of the clock. What had happened? What had set him off? I didn't know what to do. I just sat there, unable to move.

Tom was standing now, and he glared at his classmates, pointing his strong finger at them.

"Okay, you guys," he said, almost 'hissing' the words. "You be quiet and get back to work...or I'll kick your asses."

With that, he looked at me, gave me a smile, and said, "Okay Mr. U., it's all yours."

My breath somehow returned, I swallowed, and said, "Okay Tom. Thanks. Let's all get back to work."

This story doesn't have a "Hollywood" ending. Tom doesn't go on to college and become a doctor or a lawyer. He never makes it to high school, dropping out of school after that year. I saw him some years later, however, and he was doing well. He was married, had a family, and was the manager of a pizza place in a small town. Life was good.

What changed for Tom? What did I say in the phone call that made a difference? Had no other teacher called to report on what Tom was doing right, or did they only call to point out his problems? I don't know. I believe, however, that Tom felt that I was a friend, or perhaps even better, an ally, someone who thought that just maybe he could do this.

Teaching is about a lot of things. It is about lesson plans, pedagogy, standards and assessment. Most importantly it is about people. It is about building relationships and "catching them doing right". It is about having someone in your life that believes in you and can see beyond your issues and problems. We can't, in this time of increased assessment and standards, ever lose sight of the fact that we teach individuals, with individual needs. Real education can't be bought off of the rack. It has to be custom made.

Sometimes it's about taking the time to make a phone call.

18. The Power of Respect

By Joani Allen

Joani Allen taught at Spokane Falls Community College

For the past 10 years, I have had the privilege of teaching adults in a college prep program called the I-BEST. This is a 15 credit program that prepares students to either move on to more college or to venture into the world of employment. Each quarter, students came to the class with many different educational handicaps that inhibited them from being able to successfully handle regular college coursework. Many had dropped out of high school or lacked the skills to be able to compete in the job market. As a result, most students entered our program pretty beat up from life's situations and were hoping that this would be their chance – their opportunity to turn their lives around and head in a direction that they have previously only dreamed about.

After several years of teaching this course, I found a pattern that was very discouraging. The other teachers and I tried all kinds of known teaching tools to help provide success but several of the students each quarter failed to show up for class and didn't finish the course. During the first week of school, we explained many of the provisions that would help each student find success and made it very clear how they would be given opportunities to get all the help they needed to complete the course. It was baffling how so many of them would just quit. They not only would quit the course but I knew they had given up on making their dream become a reality.

I had been teaching for over 30 years and knew well how to bring encouragement and to communicate in ways that would help each student understand all that is expected for them to find success. Though I was nearing the end of my career, I wanted something more for these students. It was common each quarter for some students to come in late and not turn in assignments, or to not show up at all. Some students blamed us for requiring too much. They would tell us that it was impossible to show up for class on time. They had children to care for, busses to catch and lives to live. The reality sometimes was that they were staying out late into the evening drinking and not managing their time well. Several students told me that if we just changed our rules they would be able to pass. They would continue to tell us that they can't learn when they feel "picked" on. Our rules and consequences had been made clear, but that didn't seem to matter. What was missing? I was not willing to give up on those that had given up on themselves. Something needed to change.

It was during a conversation with a friend that I realized that many of the students had never had the opportunity to practice respect. It wasn't just about how they treated us as teachers, but how they felt about themselves that caused us not to be as effective as we wanted. On the second day of the next quarter I decided to have a workshop instead of a class day. The focus of this workshop was to discuss three concepts of respect.

1. Respect for ourselves. Self-respect fosters a desire to take responsibility for your own learning which can turn the student into an achiever and not a victim! They can feel that they have a purpose on this earth that is meant to be fulfilled. This produces an assurance of intrinsic value as a human being. People that respect themselves have a code of beliefs that they live by and that code keeps them on track so they won't quit on themselves or their dreams when the going gets tough.

2. Respect for others. Personal problems can feel overwhelming until a person sees a world filled with larger issues. Interactions with others broadens thinking. When people begin to care more about others, their capacity to care about their own

circumstances grows and they can be filled with increased hope. Perhaps most importantly, people engaged with and caring for other people often learn more about themselves.

3. Respect for the program/college. This respect is very special when a person understands how to utilize it. This involves showing respect for instructors, administrators, and support staff by respecting rules that are put into place for the benefit of everyone. This kind of respect helps develop an "attitude of gratitude" for the opportunity to attend this program or college. Fostering this type of respect helps the atmosphere change in the classroom for everyone.

I felt confident with these goals, and now the task of designing a workshop that would teach these three territories successfully began. It is one thing to come up with a good idea, but to administer something that can make a difference in the classroom is very different. I was excited for this change because I believed it might provide positive results.

My first agenda was to make sure I created an atmosphere of respect immediately in my introduction of the workshop. I wanted each student to feel safe, valued, and that our time would be productive. I began with clarifying parameters such as the use of basic manners, no gossip being tolerated and no student being laughed at. I spoke about how much all the teachers were confident that each student could be successful in this course. I made sure to say that some of them were already successful because they faced many obstacles in order to show up that day. I wanted them all to know that each person may struggle in a different area; but that we can all help each other reach those goals.

My goal was to make that day successful even if difficulties persisted the rest of the quarter.

The activities that we participated in were critical for developing respect. We started with "Find Someone Who". They were all given a page of questions. They were given a paper divided into squares. Each square contained a question like "enjoys gardening" or "sings in the shower", etc. They would mill around the room and when they found someone that met that description they would have them sign their name on the paper. This helped bring the walls down and gave everyone an awareness of the things they had in common.

The next activity was called "Interview and Introduce". They paired up and each pair was given 4 specific questions they needed to ask and answer for each other. When the questions were answered each student introduced their partner to the rest of the class as their "new friend". The feeling of community developed as students shared about each other on a deeper level and with a great deal of respect. An obvious and tangible change began to take place in the classroom. Students were conversing, sharing and laughing with each other in a way we had never seen before and it was only the second day of class. I believe that they began to feel like they would fit in and that this course wouldn't be added to their list of failed attempts toward education. They hopefully felt that learning might even be enjoyable.

The other activity was called "Success Stories". I began by asking the students to jot down on a piece of paper either "heads" or "tails". I then flipped a coin and if it landed on "heads" those who wrote down heads would pass the course and the others would not. If it landed on "tails" only those people who wrote "tails" would pass. This brought quite a reaction about how unfair this would be. We discussed for a few minutes about the injustice of this action and how it made them all feel. We then discussed about how success is really a matter of the skills and abilities that we learn and put into practice. Our success is not just a result of luck like in the coin toss. I asked them to think about two areas in their lives where they consider themselves successful and then identify the skills and abilities they used. I wanted this activity to serve as a reminder that they would not achieve much from this course through the random toss of a coin, but rather how they utilized their skills and continued to learn new ones. We applauded, cheered and acknowledged their past achievements and watched in awe as each student seemed to sit just a little bit taller in their seats.

The first workshop was an amazing success. Each person seemed more relaxed, confident and eager when the day was over. It seemed that everyone felt more accepted and valued. I began to see immediate and positive results throughout the quarter. Attendance and retention improved considerably. The focus on respect seemed to help the students be more confident about achieving their goals and more intentional about their attendance and assignment completion. They also cared more about their fellow students and how they were progressing. This definitely fostered an atmosphere in our program where students valued their own worth and that of those around them.

I realized after that day that the concept of respect and what it looks like within a classroom has a lot to do with the instructors and how they establish an "atmosphere of respect". I became more aware of how I spoke to each student, answered questions, cared about their problems and communicated in ways that made them feel valued.

There was a great day of celebration when all the students that were enrolled in the course on the first day finished successfully. I was so proud for all of these students knowing they all faced difficult challenges and not one of them quit on themselves or each other.

The next quarter Jane entered the program with many hindrances in her life skills. She had become pregnant in high school and eventually married the father of her child thinking that they would become a family. The man turned out to be very abusive and soon took off for greener pastures. Jane eventually found herself mired in a life of alcohol, drugs and more abusive relationships. Eventually, CPS came to take away her child. She had been clean for nearly 8 years when she entered into I-BEST, but was still feeling like damaged goods and not at all confident that she belonged in college. She was hesitant to talk to anyone on the first day, making the workshop a clear exposure of her damaged world. She seemed to have trouble answering any questions presented. She had communicated very clearly that she wouldn't allow anyone to touch her and that she was scared of taking tests of any kind.

I began to see a subtle change in Jane as the weeks went on. Motivated by this atmosphere of respect in the program she began to talk and share more about her life and her struggles. Soon her grades improved dramatically, she was not afraid to take tests, and she eventually began asking for hugs from the instructors because she now saw the classroom as a safe place. Jane is currently taking more college classes and is doing amazingly well. It's hard to believe that she is the same person I met a year before. Just recently we were going to do an orientation to present the I-BEST program to about 40 prospective students and Jane asked if she could speak about how the program had changed her life. It brought me to tears to see how one principle, when applied in the right circumstances, can perform miracles!

19. Mr. Swanson

By Nicole Leonard

Nicole Leonard is a teacher candidate in the School of Education at Whitworth University.

I was chosen to be in the "coolest" teacher's class at Westlake Elementary School for my upcoming fifth grade year. People knew him as the tall, skinny, young, and new teacher that everybody wanted. People always begged to be switched to his class. Luckily for me I didn't have to! The older kids said he taught with such liveliness and excitement that it was hard not to pay attention. The parents said his strategies came from a new age, and he enlightened his students but also taught in a creative way. My future teacher appeared to always encourage and support his students. He took the opportunity to get to know them personally. I even saw him playing with his kids at recess, but he also allowed students to stay in the classroom with him during recess, like when one of my older friends had a bad day. Mr. Swanson became the person we relied on, but also someone to challenge and strengthen us.

My friends and I could not wait for the first day of school with Mr. Swanson. We were all in the same class and ready to conquer fifth grade! It was looking like a fantastic year for us, and an interesting year for Mr. Swanson.

I remember the first day he taught us about handling money and savings. This could be a very difficult subject for students to understand, especially fifth graders who just want all the toys in the world. Mr. Swanson printed out "Swanson Bucks" with multiple values of 1, 5, 10, 20, 50, and 100 in "Swanson Buck" values. If we did something well, we got a raise and acquired a few bucks, but he also had the right to take away money if we did something disruptive. There was a live auction each Friday. Mr. Swanson brought some candy or toys in for each of us to bid on. One of the best prizes was the opportunity to switch seats to be next to your friend. My best friend I and saved up for this auction item. He made the economical part of life a reality in order for us to learn. He taught us how to handle money the correct way, while also incorporating classroom management. We learned that in order to get more money we had to work hard, do our job, and do our job correctly. My classmates and I also had to learn how to manage our money and save so we could spend it on what we wanted. That also led us to make priorities within our lives. Should we spend money on candy now, or save our money to switch seats in another week? This lesson was informative, but also great fun! He gave us the opportunity to be independent and make our own decisions. My friends and I remember this to this day and will probably never forget it.

Mr. Swanson always had food as a reward system. My favorite candies were the sour Starburst. One day, the class behaved really well so Mr. Swanson rewarded us, however, instead of the sour starburst he gave us each one jelly bean. I am a very picky eater, though, and had never tried jelly beans. I gave off the impression that I did not like them. So, I asked very politely and privately if I could exchange my jelly bean for a Starburst.

Mr. Swanson's face had the look of amazement and confusion that not only had I never tried a jellybean before but that I did not want to try one now. The class realized what I had asked and decided this wasn't fair. They began chanting my name, pressuring me to eat the jelly bean. Mr. Swanson did nothing. He stood there and looked at me to see what I was going to do. I let the chanting go on for a minute or so, and then I stood up for myself and said, "I'm not going to eat it if they keep doing that." A giant smile swept across Mr. Swanson's face. He then ran to his desk, grabbed a Swanson Buck and the jar of sour Starbursts. He gave me the option of choosing my favorite flavor starburst with that extra Swanson Buck. Why had he rewarded me so greatly?

As I munched on my Starburst, he retrieved the attention of the entire class, and pointed to me as a role model for resisting peer pressure. I had a huge smile on my face, not only for the rewards, but also because my teacher demonstrated how proud he was of me. I hoped that because of that incident, others in my class would feel confident enough to stand up against peer pressure. His admiration of me at that moment gave me the belief that not one single person can pressure me to do something I do not want to do. Since that instant in fifth grade, I have not given into peer pressure. In fact when I am confronted with pressure, I remember Mr. Swanson's excitement and it fuels me to stand up even stronger.

Mr. Swanson inspired me from the very first day. The way he taught and the impact he had on my life has guided me on my path through all of my school years. I hope that in my everyday life, I can influence people the way my teacher did. I hope that I can bring the same joy and excitement to learning as he did for us. Every day of my fifth grade year, Mr. Swanson gave every ounce of his energy to us, and inspired us with the utmost heart and passion.

20. Falling for Science

By Kelly Walters

Kelly Walters is a science teacher at North Central High School in Spokane, Washington.

"Today we are going to discuss a question that scientists debated 400 years ago: Do heavy objects fall faster than light objects?"

I was introducing my students to the classic physics concept that gravity will accelerate heavy objects at the same rate as light objects (ignoring air resistance, of course). The challenge here was not getting my students to memorize the fact that two different sized objects dropped simultaneously from the same height will hit at the same time. The challenge was getting them to understand the counterintuitive idea that though gravity pulls heavy objects *harder*, gravity does not pull heavy objects *faster*.

First, however, I wanted to set my students up to think about the role of air. "Let's try it by dropping a feather and a steel ball." I said. "Let's vote on which object you think will hit first." Predictably every student chose the ball. I dropped both items and, sure enough, it was not even close. The ball quickly hit the table with a thud while feather took a more leisurely path.

"So, apparently heavy objects fall faster?" I asked.

"I knew it!" exclaimed several kids who were proud of finally getting a class discussion question right.

"But that doesn't prove anything", said Steve from the back. Again, this was an expected (and hoped for) response from one of my top students.

"What do you mean?" I challenged. "The heavy object fell faster," I reminded him.

"Yeah!" exclaimed some kids who knew they were safe to be on the teacher's side of the argument.

"You changed the mass, but you also changed the air resistance," Steve observed. "You changed two variables at the same time."

"Good point Steve." I said. "How many variables should we change in an experiment, class?" I asked.

"Only one!" responded a chorus of voices, since I had drilled them about this all year.

"So, how do we eliminate air resistance?" I asked.

"Take away the air!" Several students shouted.

"True," I said. "But, we don't have the means to take away all of the air in this room right now."

"Yeah, and it would be hard to breathe." Jason shouted, followed by the hoped for laughter.

"Drop two steel balls of different mass," Sarah said

"Good thought, Sarah." I said, delighted that my lesson had been going exactly to script, even though the students thought they were helping to lead the lesson.

"Let's try it then," I said, bringing out a bigger steel ball that I just "happened" to have ready. "Before we try it, let's vote on which will hit first."

Now the students were not so sure.

"Who thinks the big ball will hit first?" I asked. I took the time to count about 15 hands so I could send the message that every opinion was valid and important to me.

"How about the small one," I asked?

No one raised their hand.

"Any takers for the small ball?" I challenged.

Stacy, sensing that this was a chance to read into the teacher's inflection and maybe be a "physics genius" for a day, took the bait and raised her hand. Jenny, her friend, slowly followed suit.

"I think they hit at the same time," Jason said, unknowingly following my script.

"Ok, who thinks they will hit at the same time?" I asked.

The rest of the class, now with surging confidence, joined Jason.

I dropped both masses and all that could be heard was a single loud thud.

"So, when we eliminate air resistance, gravity pulls both balls at the same rate," I said. "This is what Galileo did 400 years ago by dropping two different sized cannon balls out the leaning tower of Pisa".

"Was it sausage or Pepperoni?" asked Jason, again receiving his reward of scattered laughter.

"I'm not convinced," said Steve from the back row, as all heads swiveled around.

I was a little surprised by the challenge. Most kids had already written down my last proclamation as a "fact" in their science notebook and were ready to move on, but I was also pleased. This was the type of challenge that made science,

SCIENCE. Steve was thinking deeply — and deep thinking was always the objective behind the objective.

"Why not?" I asked.

"Several things," said Steve. "First of all, we only did this demonstration once. Good data requires multiple trials."

"What do you think class?" I threw back.

"He's right," admitted most students, feeling a little foolish for not thinking about it themselves first.

This was another principle that we had hammered all year.

"Good thought, Steve," I said. "Just to save time though, I can assure you that I could do this same demonstration 100 times and we would get the same result every time."

"Second of all," said Steve, obviously not done, "it doesn't make sense."

"What do you mean, it doesn't make sense?" said Sarah. "You saw it happen right in front of you and Mr. Walters told you that he could do it 500 times in a row and they would still land together. Don't you believe the teacher?"

"Oh, I believe him," Steve said, "but I don't care if he did it a thousand times in a row. It still doesn't make sense…"

"So Steve," interrupted Jason, "you aren't going to accept it even if we prove it to you?"

Suddenly, I realized that something unusual was taking place in the classroom. The kids were taking over the classroom, but not to throw paper airplanes or tease each other about who likes who. They were taking over the discussion in pursuit of learning.

So often, teachers like me are trying to get kids to answer questions that they never asked. We may demand attention, but it is not attention born out of a thirst for learning. The holy grail of teaching in one sense is to set up the stage so that the kids are asking the questions and exploring the possible answers unaware of the teacher's presence. This was one of those magic moments and so I got out of the way. I moved to a student's empty desk and sat down to watch. They hardly noticed, but just continued the dialog.

"You can give me empirical proof, but I also want logical proof," said Steve.

"What could be more logical than seeing something repeat itself 1,000 times?" said Jason.

"Jason look, if I flip a coin and it comes up heads 10 times in a row does that prove that it will always do so?" Steve asked.

"Maybe not, but if it does it 1000 times in a row, I am betting it's a two headed coin and I know that it will always be heads."

"But what if it's not a two-headed coin?" asked Steve.

"Who cares?" shouted several kids at once.

"I do," continued Steve. "If it's not a two-headed coin, then I say we just got lucky."

"Lucky a thousand times?" asked Sarah

"Yes!" said Steve emphatically

"Does gravity pull heavy things harder?" asked Steve.

"Sure does!" said Jerry, the smallest kid on the freshmen football team. "That's why Michael" (the biggest kid in the class) "squishes the breath out of me every time he tackles me."   This brought some comic relief, but the debate continued.

"Then if the earth pulls heavy things harder, then it should pull them faster too. If 200-pound Michael throws a 15-pound bowling ball as hard as he can down the lane, and 80-pound Jerry throws a 15-pound bowling ball down the lane next to it at the same time, which will hit the pins first?" Steve asked.

Most kids shouted, "Michael's ball."

Jerry though, disagreed

"Not true!" he said. "I'm now 85 pounds and my ball would hit the pins first. "

"Can you throw a 15-pound ball that fast?" asked Sarah.

"No, but Michael's ball is usually in the gutter," said Jerry.

Even Michael laughed at this.

"So, If I throw two balls and I throw one with a lot more force, won't it go faster and further?" asked Steve.

"Not if one ball is heavier," Jason said.

"But we aren't throwing bowling balls horizontally, we are dropping them vertically" said Steve.

"Does the direction matter?" asked Jason. "It's still forces acting on objects."

"Yes, it does matter," said Steve. "If I throw the ball, it stops accelerating as soon as I let go."

"So…" said Jason, not getting where this was heading.

"But when gravity pulls things down, it continues to pull," said Steve, "gravity doesn't let go, ever!"

"It keeps pulling, and pulling, and pulling. Every second it pulls harder at the heavier ball than it does on the light one. Perhaps we can't see the difference in our short demo, but give it 10 seconds, 10 minutes, or whatever of pulling and the bigger pull will eventually win out. It is only logical. Let's say we take…"

"But they still hit at the same time!" interrupted Jason. "This is about science, Steve. Science is about experiments and data and facts."

Jason then asked Jerry and Michael to come up to the front of the room. He asked Michael to stand on a chair. He then picked up Jerry, held him up to the same height as Michael on the chair and told Michael to jump. As soon as Michael jumped, Jason let go of Jerry and they both fell down to the floor, hitting at roughly the same time, and causing the whole class to break into laughter.

The experiment was crude, lacking any sort of control, but they were doing a spontaneous attempt at real science - trying to prove something to each other about the way that the world works.

"Ok, I rest my case," said Jason. "All of you who think heavy objects fall at the same rate as small objects raise your hands."

I laughed to myself, watching my students imitate my teaching method. Nearly every hand went up in the air. A few of the kids looked for my approval first.

"Who thinks the heavy objects hit first?" asked Jason.

One hand shot up without hesitation. It was Steve's hand again.

"Why don't you get it, Steve?" Jamie said, a little annoyed.

"I think he's just stubborn," said Sarah.

"Maybe I am stubborn," said Steve, "but I'm sorry, I am just not convinced."

A not-so-subtle groan rose up from the class as several students rolled their eyes.

Class was almost over and I felt it was time to step in before the stoning began.

"OK class, keep thinking about what we have learned today and you'll each have a chance to express yourselves on the test," I assured them.

At that point I wasn't done teaching about gravity. I spent several more lessons dealing with the concepts that produce the curious results of the falling body experiment. This is a more advanced concept and I didn't expect most of the students to grasp the physics of it.

To my surprise the students did fairly well on the test and most of them answered the falling masses question correctly. The falling body experiment might have worked. However, the essays revealed, that none of them could adequately explain it.

Well, except one.

And at the top of the perfect paper was a simple scribbled signature.

"Steve, period 3."

21. An Unforgettable Little Boy

By Tammy Foley

Tammy Foley is a teacher at Scootney Springs Elementary School in Othello, Washington.

Everybody said I was crazy to go out on home visits before school started, giving up what was left of my precious summer vacation, wasting my gas and my time.

"It won't make a difference anyway; it's not safe," they all said. Well, it made a difference to me. I didn't go anywhere that I didn't think was safe. If I saw wild dogs I stayed in my car until someone came out to call them in or chase them away. I usually took my Spanish-speaking assistant with me to help translate. I was a kindergarten teacher in rural Washington State with a high Mexican immigrant population that was sometimes reluctant to engage with schools and teachers. I wanted to do what I could to help them feel welcome at school. I wanted to meet my new little students on their turf where they felt comfortable before they met me in the strange world called "school".

My assistant and I pulled up to the tan and blue singlewide trailer where my little student, Joshua lived; it didn't look like anyone was home. A forgotten doll lay against the side of the house. Bright red flowers had been planted in the dirt around the front of the trailer and at the sides of the rickety wooden steps leading up to the front door. The dirt was wet so someone had recently watered the plants. We learned later that their dad had taken their one vehicle to work in the fields. We heard TV voices in Spanish as we climbed the steps and approached the front door. I knocked and a skinny little girl answered the door. She opened the door wide for us and her mother quickly stood behind her. My assistant explained that I was Joshua's kindergarten teacher and we were here to meet him. His mom lowered the volume on the novella they were watching and invited us in. I saw a little black-haired, brown-eyed boy sitting on the sofa and knew it must be Joshua. I went over to the sofa and introduced myself to Joshua, putting my hand out for him to take as my assistant continued to chat with the mom. Joshua wouldn't take my hand, but turned his head shyly and looked down at the sofa. I recognized his older brother from school and asked about his summer.

The trailer was small and very crowded. The living room held a pair of handmade bunk beds against the wall in addition to the sofa and TV. A round, white plastic patio table with white plastic chairs was in the far corner by a small kitchen. The mom explained that the home had only 2 bedrooms so Joshua and his older brother slept on the bunk beds in the living room. We stayed about thirty minutes, answering the mom's questions and trying to get Joshua to tell us about what he liked/disliked. He remained quiet throughout our visit, looking down shyly when we asked him any questions directly. I was worried he was going to cry on the first day of school and I desperately wanted him to feel more comfortable with me. I gave him a small bag with crayons, paper, pencils, candy, and a toy car. He opened his mouth in surprise with a grin that showed two rows of bright white baby teeth and dimpled cheeks. He took the bag and quietly examined everything in it. I could only hope he would be okay once he came to school.

The morning of the first day of school dawned sunny and hot. I had butterflies in my stomach, worrying about Joshua and the other children who seemed reluctant to come to school. I wondered how many would cry and for how long, but I need not have worried about Joshua. His older brother brought him to our classroom, led Joshua to his cubby where he took a folded piece of paper out of his backpack, and then shyly left him at the door.

"I am so glad to see you this morning, Joshua. You're going to be just fine", I said to him, putting out my hand.

Joshua handed me the folded paper. I opened it to reveal a colorful drawing of his family, all standing in a row. I knew it was from him, but it was so good I thought his older brother must have helped him.

"Wow," I said. "This is a great picture of your family."

He glanced back down the hall in the direction his brother had gone and then up at me with watery brown eyes, his lips wobbling, but he took my hand and let me lead him to his table where I had laid out paper and crayons. I soon discovered that he liked to draw! Not only did he like to draw, but he was very good at it. He didn't draw in simple stick figures and "m" shaped birds like most 5-year-olds. His people had bodies and wore clothes and had facial expressions and were standing in tall grass with big loopy flowers. There were bushy red apple trees with stems in the apples and fat green leaves stuck on the sides and chubby birds with round heads, yellow beaks, and fluffy wings flying overhead. There were red and black race cars with numbers on their hoods and smoke coming out the back. All through that fall Joshua continued to smile shyly, but he drew and drew and drew, filling all of the pages of his writing journal with simple sentences and beautiful illustrations. During our November parent-teacher conference, I shared his writing journal with his mom. She was so proud to hear that her son's handwriting and drawing were so exceptional for his age.

"Maybe he will illustrate books or become an architect when he grows up?" I said to her.

His mom's eyes shone and she rubbed her chest, imagining such a future for her son.

In December, we had our class Christmas program. The children sang traditional holiday songs for their parents, I passed out treats and small presents for each of the kids and we all enjoyed cookies and hot chocolate. I mingled among the families, chatting with everyone, taking photographs for the end of the year memory books. I asked the parents to gather up their children on their laps as a finale to our Christmas program. I darkened the room so only our Christmas lights were twinkling in the room and all together we sang, "Silent Night". I looked around the room at all of my little students, snuggled so cozily on their parents laps. It was cold and snowing outside, but inside we were all so warm and comfy and peaceful together, all of us full of holiday happiness. And there was Joshua, sitting on his mom's lap, his back resting against her; his mom's cheek resting against the side of his head, their fingers intertwined as she gently rocked him. It was so perfect and beautiful. It was a moment frozen in time for me.

I don't remember when the phone rang later that year or even who called me. All I remember is hearing, "One of your students died."

"What?" I asked, my lists of students running through my mind.

"There was a car accident. Your little Joshua was ejected and... he died at the scene."

When I was able to piece together what happened I learned that with no car to collect Joshua from a sleep over his mom had asked a relative to bring him home. The relative had crossed the center line and they were hit head on. Joshua wasn't wearing a seat belt and went through the windshield. There was nothing the paramedics could do for him. Every year since then at our Christmas program, when all of the children are nestled in their parent's laps, I look around and I think of Joshua, with his big brown eyes, black hair and dimples, and I remember his beautiful drawings that told of all the things that he needed to say.

22. The Difficult Teacher

By Lauren Drury

Lauren Drury is a teacher candidate in the School of Education at Whitworth University.

I remember clearly walking to fourth period on the first day of seventh grade filled with fear. The brand new experience of junior high school was the understandable cause of my nerves on this afternoon. The beginning of the day had gone remarkably well, but now a sense of apprehension had descended on the group of new friends I had made on this first day as we headed from lunch to our first algebra class. We had heard rumors about the teacher in whose classroom we would be kept for the next fifty-five minutes. Older students had told us that her classes were difficult and required a lot of work, and now we were scared. However, this was before we learned that a challenging teacher was certainly not synonymous with a bad teacher. Over the three years that my peers and I had the opportunity to work with this teacher, we learned that quite the opposite was true.

In fact, it did not take us long to realize that our year with this teacher would be different from what we had expected. Walking into her classroom, we were overwhelmed with the sheer magnitude of Star Wars-related objects that filled this small portable. Action figures lined the perimeter diligently watching over the nervous seventh grade algebra students who took in this room with awe.

Though we grew to love this teacher, the class was not perfect right away. Our first test did not go well and our teacher had a talk with us about what it meant to take a rigorous course. This class would be challenging as we made the leap from elementary school math to algebra 1, but she let us know that if we were willing to work for it, she was going to get us through the year. And get us through the year she did, and the year after that and the year after that.

The year had its challenges for us as students and for our teacher as this was the first time that an algebra class at our school was made up entirely of seventh graders. Through the struggles along the way however, our teacher managed to keep us afloat. She was incredibly knowledgeable when it came to mathematics and she effectively taught us the many mathematical concepts we needed to know.

Though we perceived her as brilliant, this was not the only reason that our teacher was special, someone we admired, trusted, and *wanted* to work for. She showed us that she cared about us as individuals, not only as students that sat in her class for an hour each day. She listened to us. She shared in our joys and she shared in our sorrows and there was never too little time to share an occasional story or joke.

We learned from this teacher outside her familiar portable just as much as we did inside of it. Her passion was manifested in the countless hours she spent helping with projects for the betterment of our school and the student body. Working at our school was not simply a job for this teacher but rather a passionate way of life. She demonstrated the meaning of serving others and she encouraged us to get involved and to do the same.

I was saddened to find out in my eighth grade year that she would not be my geometry teacher. This minor obstacle, however, did not stop me from seeing her every day. I continued to eat lunch in her portable with all of my friends. Above all she was our teacher, but she cared about us as fellow human beings and she was there whenever we needed support. Though some of us only saw her for the brief thirty minute lunch, we knew beyond the shadow of a doubt that she would always be there if we needed her. I had gone from being an anxious seventh grader to being a proud member of this teacher's figurative fan club.

I had the privilege of having this teacher once again in ninth grade. Algebra 2 was challenging and at times I doubted my abilities. The importance of the impact this teacher had on my life came to an apex one day during a test. I always did my tests very slowly as I was overly worried about making mistakes. She allowed the class a couple of extra days to finish and when these days were over, I had yet to complete my test. She understandably told me that time was up as I had been given ample time to finish. I was worried not that I had failed the test, I knew what I was doing despite being overly cautious, but rather that I had disappointed this teacher who I admired so much. Later she talked to me and told me that she believed in my ability to finish the tests in the allotted time. After all, I had always done well in her class. My goal for the next test was to finish in time and when I did and aced the test, she celebrated with me.

It was not just the good score on the test that we celebrated but rather what this score reflected. I had achieved something I had not allowed myself to think possible and I showed positive growth in my test taking abilities and my learning. After all, our understanding of the material meant far more to her than a letter grade on a piece of paper.

Her display of confidence in me and the lasting impact it had meant more to me than she could have imagined. Deep down I always knew that I was a capable mathematics student but this was the push I needed to bolster my confidence in my mathematical abilities. I was able to carry this confidence with me through high school and into university math classes.

However, her impact transcended mathematical boundaries. I saw, as a future educator, the potential to make an impact on the lives of students in an inspiring way through this teacher. We got through challenging mathematical concepts not simply because of her ability to teach us academics but because she cared. We wanted to work for her because she worked for us. She listened to our triumphs and mishaps, but not only that, she shared with us. She knew us, but we also knew her.

We all knew that when the stool that sat in the corner of the room came out it was time for a story. We learned from her not only the quadratic formula and how to foil like champions, but also how to be good human beings and members of society. She led by example as she guided us through the somewhat rocky terrain of algebra and life as junior high school students.

Capturing in words the essence of this teacher and what she meant to the students whose lives she touched is a formidable task. While reflecting on this teacher and the time we spent in her classroom, a friend underscored my feelings. She aptly described having this incredible teacher as "an experience." From the moment we walked into her classroom on the first day of seventh grade until the day we bade each other tearful farewells when we left ninth grade, our interactions with this teacher were indeed an experience that impacted each and every one of us. This teacher taught us, challenged us, embraced us and guided us. Sometimes her class was indeed difficult just as we had been told, but for those students who had the privilege of learning from this teacher in the small Star Wars filled portable, we knew that with her help the force was always with us.

23. The Sting

By Dave Stenersen

Dave Stenersen is the principal at Northwood Middle School in Mead, Washington.

The middle school and junior high years are full of many challenges. Students are going through intense physical, social and emotional changes that make motivation and learning difficult.

Once in a while there needs to be an event that breaks the routine and really captures their attention.

The year was 1985, and I was a middle school math teacher at Mead Jr. High. I taught 7th and 8th grade math, but my favorite class was an advanced 7th grade math class. They were polite, funny and, for 7th graders, very self-assured. On this particular day in May, students entering my 4th period math class expected a "business as usual" type of day. I was wearing a tie, which meant I was dressed up, and students could sense I was a bit nervous. They did not know the young lady who was also dressed nicely, sitting at my desk. The class was more quiet than usual as they took their seats. I waited until everyone was sitting down before explaining the day's unusual opportunity.

I introduced our guest, Miss Wirth, a doctoral student from WSU. She had chosen our school and this class in particular, to be involved in her doctoral research. I asked the class if they would be willing to help her, and waited until there was an overwhelming "yes". Without any further explanation, I asked Miss Wirth to give an overview of her thesis, describe her research and explain to the class how they would be involved. With much excitement and pride, these advanced math students worked hard to listen well and make sure Miss Wirth knew that they were the best possible class for her study. The room was silent, and every eye was on our guest.

The explanation given by Miss Wirth to the class contained dozens of multi-syllable words, of which only a few were recognizable. Although everyone was confused, none of these advanced 7th grade math students wanted to appear nonexceptional. Nothing was asked, although everyone wondered what in the world she was talking about. However, everyone in the room did seem to get the general drift, which had to do with "*a powerful correlation between purposeful, positive mental activity and the successful completion of an event.*" By asking some clarifying questions to Miss Wirth, we made clear the premise of her thesis, which was something like "If we spend time imagining an event happening, it is much more likely to happen."

Miss Wirth explained why she was in our class. She wanted me to randomly choose one student. That student would identify 5 things they wanted to happen. Examples she gave were "like doing well on a test, or winning a baseball game." I was to write those 5 things on the board while she recorded them in her research log. After the five events were identified and written on the board, she wanted the entire class to spend 90 seconds as a group, silently imagining those things happening, and then she would track the results. It appeared she was hopeful that results from this class would confirm her thesis, as she said had happened in her earlier research.

Making sure that the entire class was on board, I asked if we were ready and willing to proceed. Very politely, but with electric excitement, all the students were eager to continue. I told Miss Wirth, that without looking, I would drop a pencil on the names of these students in my grade-book. The student whose name was under or closest to the sharp point of my pencil lead would be the random student who would choose the five events. She agreed that method was random. I made sure that the students would all commit to this process regardless whether they were randomly picked or not. After a glacially slow pause wherein I made eye contact with each student, the entire class was on pins and needles to see on which student's name the pencil landed.

"Brent Busby" I called, allowing several seconds to elapse after dropping the pencil. The combination of their disappointment with not being chosen themselves, but delighted with Brent being the choice, created the first sense of an unruly disruption. I quickly got everyone back to "advanced-student" behavior. Every student was watching Brent, wondering what would happen next. Brent was popular, athletic, smart, but he could also be a smart mouth. Most students thought he was a perfect choice. What might he do?

It was obvious that I was thinking the same thing as I introduced Brent to our guest, Miss Wirth. My non-verbal "you better behave yourself" looks and comments towards Brent were not hard to miss. Brent came forward and politely shook hands with our guest. She asked him to please come up with 5 events "*like doing well on a test*" for her research. She asked if he was ready, and said he was. The class breathlessly waited for his first "event."

"I want a Swedish Chef to come into our room," he said in his secure, smart-mouth voice.

I got up and walked towards him as he continued "and I want his name to be Matt."

I was visibly upset, and students were thinking that even Brent had pushed this too far. There was major tension in the air. The class loved it.

I said all the appropriate things about being respectful, not wrecking our guest's research project, throwing in additional non-verbal cues, but Brent was un-phased.

"I was the one chosen, and this is what I want." He said, with heavy emphasis on the "I."

This sounded logical, and the class quickly saw Brent's position. Most of them seemed to side with this stance. I looked embarrassed as I asked Miss Wirth what to do. She appeared shaken, but seemed like she wasn't going to be flustered. She said "Brett is correct. He was the one chosen," and asked him to continue.

Brent continued, "I want him to bring us all cookies. Chocolate chip cookies."

Chris, another boy in the back of the room shouted out "Not chocolate chip! I like chocolate no-bake cookies. Make them chocolate no-bake cookies"

Brent got a bigger smile, turned to Miss Wirth and said, "I want a Swedish chef named Matt to bring us chocolate, no-bake cookies."

I got up from my chair, gave Brent a menacing look, gave Miss Wirth an "I'm so sorry" look, and sat back down.

Miss Wirth looked up from her notes, and asked "How many cookies?"

Brent looked around the room, silently counted everyone, and said "Thirty-three."

Once again, from the back of the room, Chris shouted out "No! Make it thirty-three and a third."

Brent turned to Miss Wirth and in his self-assured, smart-mouthed voice said, "I want him to bring thirty-three and a third chocolate no-bake cookies."

I got up again, but sat back down, as I had already made my point, and I knew Brent was going to do whatever he wanted.

Miss Wirth said, "I think that is 4 events. We need one more."

Brent continued, "I want him to be wearing purple shoelaces."

I bolted up, and was obviously very upset with this, but Brent would not back down. He suggested that the class vote, and said that I could choose the other shoelace color. I chose black. We voted. Students who wanted the shoelaces to be black raised their hands. Those who wanted purple raised their hands. The results were 2 votes for black, 29 for purple.

Miss Wirth asked me to write the five events on the board. With Brent's help I wrote:

A Swedish chef enters the room.

His name is Matt.

He brings us cookies (thirty-three and a third no-bake chocolate cookies).

He is wearing purple shoelaces.

Brent said the list of events was correct, and he sat down.

Miss Wirth was visibly upset, but continued on. She asked everyone to close their eyes and imagine a Swedish chef named Matt, entering our room with thirty-three and a third chocolate no-bake cookies. She reminded us we also needed to imagine him wearing purple shoelaces. The class settled down, and for 90 seconds there was silence as thirty-one seventh graders imagined Swedish Matt with purple shoelaces coming into our classroom.

After the ninety seconds was over, the intense drama gave way to a quiet aftershock. Miss Wirth excused herself and sat at my desk. She told the class she was working on a biorhythm for each student. Nobody had a clue what she meant, but nothing was said. We began correcting homework. Students became concerned that we had wrecked Miss Wirth's research.

A student asked Miss Wirth, "What if part of this comes true? What if someone named Matt comes in our room?"

Miss Wirth responded that all five of the events needed to happen for her thesis to be validated. I asked Miss Wirth if this wrecked everything, and she bravely smiled, saying that there would be times it doesn't work, and this would be one of those times. The class knew we were now wasting Miss Wirth's time, but we needed to finish the job. Miss Wirth made sure that the research environment was not contaminated. She made sure the intercom was turned off, so nobody could be "listening in" and send us a Swedish chef named Matt. We confirmed that it was turned off, and had been turned off the whole period.

The classroom door opened, and every eye looked up to see who was coming in. It was Mrs. Smick, one of the school counselors, to see a student. I told her the student she needed couldn't leave until the end of the period, which was still 11 minutes away, because that would contaminate the research. Mrs. Smick was not happy to stay in the room, but she did.

As the minutes ticked off, students worked on their new assignment, with most of the previous events becoming just a weird story that could be told that evening at dinner. Students kept glancing at the door, just in case. Mrs. Smick was looking at the clock.

With three minutes left in the period there was a knock at the door. A young man in a chef's hat, carrying a silver platter, opened the door and walked in. Embroidered on his white chef's jacket was the name "Matt." The entire class looked in disbelief. At almost the exact same second, everyone noticed his purple shoelaces. A girl sitting nearby looked at me and said, "You set us up!" After denying any set-up, I reminded her that they all voted on the shoelace color. As she realized it was true, her eyes got big and she shrieked "Oh my gosh! We did!"

The chef with the platter began to speak. He had a Swedish accent. I asked him what was under the platter. He showed us all and said, with a Swedish accent, "Cookies. Chocolate, no-bake cookies." I asked him how many, and he counted them. "Thirty-three and a tiny bit more." He said.

The bell rang as the chef finished counting. As students began leaving for lunch, he gave each a chocolate no-bake cookie. Students were in shock. I heard one say as she left, "That was a miracle"

I am sure all the students eventually found out exactly how this "miracle" happened but Brent and Chris kept their involvement secret for days. We certainly broke the routine that day and captured everyone's attention.

Just another weird day in middle school.

24. Happy Father's Day

By Dr. Dennis Sterner

Dennis Sterner is a former high school teacher and was Dean of the School of Education at Whitworth University for 23 years.

Tim was a student in one of my eight grade science classes where he was a consistent, well-behaved B+ student. The parts of the class that he liked best were the demonstrations that I did and the hands-on experiments that I had students do. Frequently he would come in after school and ask if he could try a demonstration with the equipment that I used or to work more on a lab that was done earlier in the day. I'd make sure that he didn't get involved in anything dangerous and that he knew how to use the equipment and then just let him go while I helped other students, proctored make-up tests or graded papers.

Over time I got to know Tim pretty well and enjoyed his enthusiasm and the conversations that we had. I learned that he and his brother lived with their mom who worked as a waitress/bar-maid. I met her at an open house one night and she seemed to be a very caring mother who worked hard to support her two boys and make ends meet. She wanted the kids to do well in school and made sure that they studied and did their homework. Tim never mentioned his dad so I was unsure if he was ever in the picture.

The school year ended about a week and a half into June and on the last day of school Tim came up after class, handed me a card, said thanks for letting him come in after school and wished me a good summer. I wished the same for him and placed the card on my desk along with several other cards and small gifts that students had given me that day. When the final bell rang and the kids all left the building I was in my room putting things away and getting ready to head home. I decided to open the cards on my desk and one by one, enjoyed the kind and sometimes humorous comments made by my students.

Then I opened Tim's card. As soon as I pulled it out of the envelope, I had a multitude of feelings that to this day are hard to describe but could, I guess, be summed up as "I never knew." What I never knew was that to Tim, I had become a father figure, a person who was there for him in the absence of his real father, day after day, throughout the year. The card that Tim gave me that day said "Happy Father's Day" and was just signed, "Tim." Father's day would take place the following Sunday and although at that time I had no children of my own, I certainly thought of Tim and hoped he was doing okay. He moved away that summer and I never saw him again.

What this experience proved to me was that we sometimes impact the lives of people in ways that we never realize. I was a young teacher when Tim was in my class and never thought of myself as a father figure to any of my students, but that experience was one that I have never forgotten; it changed me and the way that I related to the kids in my class. I tried to be much more in touch with where they were in life and tried to be conscious of my role in their lives. None of my students ever gave me a father's day card again, but the one that Tim gave me is still stuck away in a file in my house.

Tim, I hope that life has been good to you and that you have been a father figure to some children in your life.

25. The Gift of Teaching: Learning As a Way of Life

By Dr. Harvey B. Alvy

Harvey Alvy is a former elementary principal and is a Professor of Educational Leadership, Emeritus, at Eastern Washington University.

Teachers on their very first and very last day share a common gift - they hear the eager voices of students.

While serving as an elementary school principal, I hired Kathy G., a veteran teacher with outstanding recommendations. I was excited to have Kathy join our learning community. However, following the hire she said something that concerned me.

"I've taught second grade for the last twenty years, know the curriculum, and really enjoy that age group. If you have a second grade opening, I would love to take it."

I thought, "Oops! Is Kathy a burnout case who just wants to recycle her old lessons and sail into the sunset without challenging herself or her students?" Since we had a second grade opening it was only fair to discuss the position with her. Politely, I expressed my concerns. Kathy assured me that teaching, and the challenges of second graders rejuvenated her each year. I was skeptical. However, based on excellent recommendations and credentials Kathy deserved to have her request honored. Quickly I learned that my initial concerns were mistaken. Kathy was made for second grade.

Kathy had an enormous capacity for growth. During our first pre-observation conference she asked me to observe a cooperative learning lesson. Kathy reflected that in previous years she had only touched the surface with cooperative learning. She wanted to go deeper, giving students more ownership and independence. As Kathy shared ideas it became clear that I was in the presence of a master teacher.

Two days later I observed her cooperative learning science lesson. The lesson empowered the class. Kathy's students debated "hypotheses" in groups and shared conclusions with the whole class. As Kathy circulated among the various independent groups

I was struck by her focus and listening skills; and the student comments dictated her movements and responses.

The following day I looked forward to our post-observation conference. What would Kathy have to say? Her comments about teaching and the specific lesson were profound, and refreshingly candid.

Kathy shared her "fear" of letting students have too much control of a lesson. She felt a little guilty about being "just a fly on the wall" during much of the cooperative lesson. Yes, she watched students interact and at times facilitated the work of different table groups. However, Kathy was not actively steering the lesson's direction and stated that this was difficult and a bit discomforting. She knew this feeling was based on her initial training and insightfully acknowledged the challenge of shedding one's early habits.

Additionally, Kathy shared her reflections related to patterns of learning observed while checking for student understanding. She brought samples of student work to our conference to reinforce her points. Kathy admonished herself (unfairly!) concerning some confusion related to lesson directions and how students performed individual cooperative learning responsibilities. I reminded Kathy that her thoughtful lesson preparation and intentional directions enabled students to raise important issues, draw insightful conclusions, and respectfully interact with one another. Her work was impressive!

I then raised a few questions:

"What surprised you about the lesson?"

"Did you meet your goals?"

"Are there particular students that you would like to talk about?"

References
Bennis, W., & Nanus, B. (1985). *Leaders: The strategies for taking charge.* New York, NY: Harper & Row.
Hattie, J. (2009). *Visible learning: A synthesis of over 800 meta-analysis related to achievement.* New York, NY: Routledge.

Author's Note

I'm sitting at my desk, reading my course evaluations. No matter how long I have taught, I always get nervous reading these. I take my position as an educator seriously, and I want to do well in preparing my teaching candidates. I want them to be prepared, not only with the current research-based theories and concepts, but for the realities of the classroom. There are many good comments on the evaluations, and many good suggestions as well. I will try to implement many of these next semester. There are also comments that I have come to expect. These show up on almost all of my course evaluations. My students enjoy the stories I tell.

They talk about the importance of the stories. It is the stories that make the course-work "real". It is the stories that prepare them for what they might really face. The course textbooks are very good. They provide great information and detailed research and information. But it is the stories, my students tell me, that give the concepts life. No longer is it about a research conducted somewhere else with anonymous subjects. No longer is it about a classroom somewhere with a teacher they don't know. The former students in my stories become real to them because they were real to me. My teaching candidates feel like they know Cory and Jesse, two former students that impacted my life and my career greatly. It is through my stories that my university students begin to actually see themselves in the front of a classroom, looking out at their students, looking for their own Cory or Jesse.

Reading the comments on my evaluations, impressed again by the impact of the stories I tell in my courses, I thought how all teachers have their stories. We all have the interactions with students that are memorable. They are memorable because of the breakthroughs and growth we get to witness. They are memorable because of the strength and resilience exhibited by children in very difficult situations. They are memorable because of the joy, laughter, tears and sorrow that change us and the way we teach.

I reached out to several colleagues, asking them to send me a story or two about something memorable that happened in their classrooms. This request spread to others through word of mouth. I began to receive stories from people I didn't know. I also invited my university students to contribute stories about teachers that influenced them. I didn't ask for stories on a specific theme; just for stories about something memorable.

A theme immerged, however. Almost all of the stories are about relationships. The relationship between teacher and student is at the heart of effective teaching. The stories in this book clearly reflect that. Standards are needed. Assessment is necessary. The key to education, however, is the relationship between teacher and student. We have to know our students to know how to apply the standards, how to instill motivation for learning, and to know the proper timing, and method, for effective assessment.

Without relationship, the stories in this book don't exist. All of us have been impacted, positively or negatively, by a teacher. We have learned, or failed to learn, because of a teacher. It is the teachers that took the time to get to know us, to care for us, that pushed us forward, perhaps further than we thought possible.

I hope the stories in this book inspire you. I hope they are confirming to those of you thinking about a career in education. I hope they help you remember a teacher that took the time to know you, not just teach you.

You are invited to send me your classroom stories if you would like to contribute to the next edition of *Head of the Class*. You may help encourage and inspire current teachers in the field and those preparing to embark in this most noble profession.

Contact me at drjuhlenkott@gmail.com.

About Christa Prentiss

Christa Prentiss graduated with a Bachelor of Arts from Whitworth University in 2014. She is currently pursuing a career in health sciences and working on a number of commissioned art projects.

Christa infuses her art into everything she does. Her venture into the area of pre-medicine, an area not appearing to be closely aligned with art, has proven to be a complimentary discipline. Her interest in science, combined with her artistic talent has allowed her to provide clarity and focus in her oil paintings of the human figure.

When she is not applying graphite to paper Christa likes to get lost in national parks, discover new 90s music to play on her guitar, and avoid trees on the ski slope.

About Jim Uhlenkott

Like many of us, Jim has had many "careers" and done many things. He taught for 18 years in public education, teaching Title 1 reading at the junior high level, and at the elementary level he has taught grades 3, 4 and 6, as well as one year of elementary music, where he instituted the Preschool Marching Band (another story for another time). Jim as also taught at the university level, teaching courses at Gonzaga University, Eastern Washington University, and in his current position at Whitworth University. He has also been a summer camp counselor, assistant director and director, and directed a summer camp for diabetic youth. He and his family lived in Slovakia twice. The first time was in the summer of 1991 where he toured Eastern Europe as a bass player for Janny Grein ministries. The second was in 1998 and 1999 when he and his wife, Malinda, taught a leadership course for young adults.

Jim and Malinda have been married for over 40 years; have four grown children and eight grandchildren (so far). They live in Mead, just north of Spokane, Washington.